IMAGES
of America

LAKE JUNALUSKA

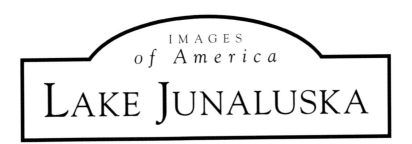

IMAGES
of America

LAKE JUNALUSKA

William E. King

ARCADIA
PUBLISHING

Published by Arcadia Publishing
Charleston, South Carolina

Printed in the United States of America

Library of Congress Control Number: 2009939157

For all general information contact Arcadia Publishing at:
Telephone 843-853-2070
Fax 843-853-0044
E-mail sales@arcadiapublishing.com
For customer service and orders:
Toll-Free 1-888-313-2665

Visit us on the Internet at www.arcadiapublishing.com

*To four generations of the King family who have
worked at and enjoyed Lake Junaluska*

CONTENTS

Acknowledgments   6

Introduction   7

1.   A Dream Fulfilled   9

2.   The Dream Expands   33

3.   A Focus on Christian Education   59

4.   A Tradition of Music   73

5.   Having Fun at Lake Junaluska   81

6.   Recreation and Youth Activities   101

7.   Homes With a Story   121

ACKNOWLEDGMENTS

With a professional career as a university archivist preserving institutional history and directing researchers in the use of records and manuscripts, I am well aware of the cooperative effort inherent in any publication. I am most grateful to fellow Junaluska residents and friends who loaned photographs and helped with identifications. Their assistance, encouragement, and shared memories made the project fun. Tom Harkins helped with the use of the Mason Crum papers in the Duke University Archives. Vicki Hyatt provided access to the photographic files of the Waynesville, North Carolina newspaper, the *Mountaineer*. This book would not have been possible without the labor of past directors and staff of the Heritage Center at Lake Junaluska who collected and preserved records and photographs of the Lake Junaluska Assembly. Current part-time staff members at the Heritage Center—Art Swarthout and Rachael Suggs, and especially Ashley Calhoun and acting director A. V. Huff—helped bring the project to fruition. Marie Metcalf provided the few modern photographs in the book.

The history of Lake Junaluska is available in a variety of published sources, but I am very much indebted to *The Story of Lake Junaluska* (1950) by my valued friend Mason Crum. Published pamphlets by Diane Stanton-Rich, the late Joe Lasley, and reference aids by Bill Lowry on deposit in the Heritage Center were particularly helpful.

Modern publishing—and especially a compilation of photographic images—is dependent on individuals with technical knowledge. I have a functional knowledge of technological aids but am heavily dependent on those with much more skill in understanding and making the necessary equipment work. This book would not have been completed without the much-appreciated assistance of my wife, Helen B. King, and Will Crenshaw, a member of the IT staff at Lake Junaluska Assembly. When the need for additional assistance became apparent, Clifton Metcalf, Junaluska resident and vice chancellor for advancement and external affairs at Western Carolina University, directed me to the Mountain Heritage Center at nearby Western Carolina University. Scott Philyaw, director of the Mountain Heritage Center, graciously let me use its facilities, and Peter Koch (education associate), Christie Osborne (project coordinator/DigitalHeritage.org), Scott Chamness (student assistant), and Sona Norton (office manager), directed me through the process.

This book is not an authorized, sponsored study. The selection of photographs, interpretation, and errors are mine alone. It is compiled with a demonstrated loyalty to Lake Junaluska. I was born one April, brought to Lake Junaluska the following June, and have never missed a summer. My father's employment as executive secretary of the board of education of the Western North Carolina Conference of the United Methodist Church brought our family to Junaluska every summer. My wife and I built our retirement home on Littleton Road early in my career, and Junaluska became our permanent residence in 2005.

Unless otherwise noted, all images appear courtesy of the Heritage Center, Lake Junaluska.

INTRODUCTION

Lake Junaluska is located in Haywood County, North Carolina, near Waynesville, within sight of the Blue Ridge Parkway and next door to the Great Smoky Mountains National Park. As an institution it is the historic assembly ground, at its inception in 1913, of the Methodist Episcopal Church, South, now known as the United Methodist Church. First called the Southern Assembly, it became the Lake Junaluska Assembly in 1929. Initially a summer meeting place, it now operates year-round under the auspices of the Lake Junaluska Conference and Retreat Center. It is governed by a board of directors and the quadrennial conference of the Southeastern Jurisdiction of the United Methodist Church. Geographically its locus is in the nine states from Mississippi to Virginia, including Florida, Tennessee, and Kentucky, but it hosts conferences and draws conferees from throughout the United States and the world. In area, the assembly grounds total approximately 1,200 acres, which include church-owned conference facilities and hotels and private inns and family dwellings surrounding a 250-acre lake. In 2013, the Lake Junaluska Assembly will celebrate its centennial anniversary.

But Lake Junaluska is much more than a geographical location. Mason Crum, a summer resident from 1920 to 1980 and professor of religion at Duke University, characterizes Lake Junaluska as "an idea, not merely a place or an institution." He develops the concept in his book, *The Story of Lake Junaluska*, published in 1950, which is a personal account of the Junaluska experience. Bringing his concept up to date, Junaluska is a retreat not only for those attending a variety of scheduled conferences, but also one for families and guests. It is a place of inspiration recalled by many a minister and layperson as a special place of Christian commitment. Once called the "Summer Capital of Southern Methodism," it attracts visitors from around the world all year long. Its founders sought to create a religious institution in the region that was in the tradition of successful gathering places like Ocean Grove in New Jersey, Northfield in Massachusetts, Winona Lake in Indiana, and the renowned Chautauqua Lake in New York. They succeeded in attracting the best preachers and leaders of the church for inspiration and instruction along with entertainers to complement "the best in recreation, outdoor living, and culture," to quote Crum. And it is a place of rest, increasingly important in a fast-paced world.

Historical context obviously influenced the development of the Methodist Assembly, which was successfully launched in 1913. World War I and its aftermath slowed growth and complicated financing. As the future brightened, the Great Depression and then World War II again created uncertainty. However, the Lake Junaluska Methodist Assembly triumphed over bankruptcy, provided sought-after programs for the church, and had the leadership to rebuild and grow through the 1950s, 1960s, and 1970s. All was certainly not easy. The progressivism of its founders was carried forward in Christian education, support for missions, and training generations of clergy and lay leaders, but it was not so progressive across the board. Acceptance of women in positions of leadership grew, but developed slowly. Racial integration was accomplished after a long struggle. Some speakers and conferences were needlessly controversial. In short, the history of the assembly was not separate from the trends and experiences of the 20th-century church and nation.

This book of vintage photographs is not a true history with tested generalizations and careful analysis. It is a collection of images covering the period roughly from 1913 to 1985. It is a visual interpretation of the Junaluska experience by the author. The story is constrained both by the number of photographic images that have survived and the reproducible quality of those images. The bane of every archivist and historian is unidentified and undated photographs, which unfortunately abound. But an interesting visual record does exist. That record clearly demonstrates the development of the "Junaluska idea." Facilities and programs evolved to provide venues for inspiration, instruction, entertainment, and rest. As the founders desired, activities centered not only around Stuart Auditorium and Shackford Hall, but also around the lake and in the context of the surrounding mountains. Junaluska is a place, but thankfully it is more than a place.

One

A DREAM FULFILLED

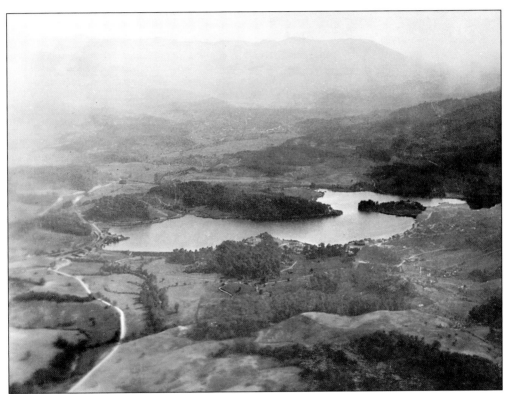

AERIAL VIEW OF LAKE JUNALUSKA, C. 1920. Religious assembly grounds were popular in Massachusetts (Northfield), Indiana (Winona Lake), New Jersey (Ocean Grove), and New York (Chautauqua Lake) in the late 19th century. Southern Methodists, led by Bishop James Atkins and George R. Stuart, sought to rectify the lack of the new institution in the South. Although members of the Sunday School Board, these two leaders of the Methodist Episcopal Church, South won support for the assembly concept through discussion and action at several missionary conferences. In June 1913, the Second General Missionary Conference of the church held the first meeting at the recently laid out Southern Assembly grounds, later named Lake Junaluska Assembly, near Waynesville, North Carolina. The distinctive physical feature of the grounds of the Assembly was a 250-acre lake, which added the pleasure of "play with a purpose" to the attractions of inspiration and education. The identifying slogan for the Lake Junaluska Assembly for many years was the "Summer Capital of Southern Methodism."

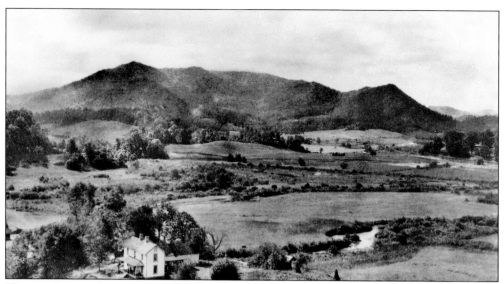

HOMESTEAD AND RICHLAND CREEK C. 1912. Richland Creek Valley, some of the best farmland in Haywood County, became the site of the Methodist assembly grounds. Located west of the renowned resort town of Asheville and near Waynesville, North Carolina, the site capitalized on the pleasing climate and beauty of the southern Appalachian Mountains later widely known by the creation of the nearby Blue Ridge Parkway and the Great Smoky Mountains National Park.

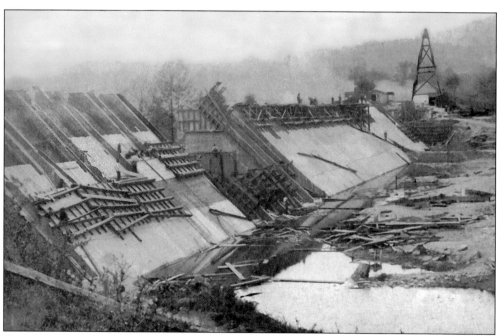

CONSTRUCTION ON THE DAM C. 1912. Begun in 1911, the dam was completed by the time of the first conference at the assembly grounds in June 1913, but the lake was only partially full.

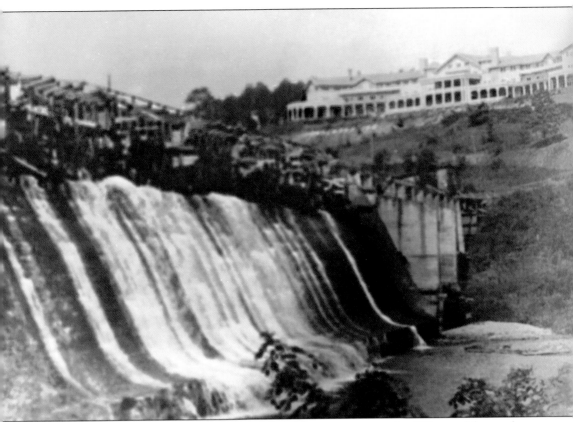

COMPLETED DAM. The dam added the recreational opportunities of a 250-acre lake to the beauty of mountain scenery as a physical draw to complement inspiration and education at the Methodist assembly grounds. Above is a rare view of the Junaluska Inn on the hill above the dam. The inn was first used in 1917 but lost by fire in 1918.

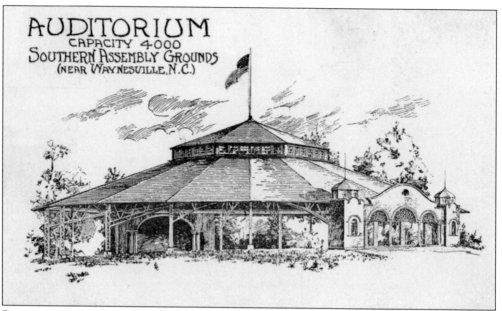

AUDITORIUM
CAPACITY 4000
SOUTHERN ASSEMBLY GROUNDS
(NEAR WAYNESVILLE, N.C.)

PROPOSED AUDITORIUM C. 1912. Open air, circular auditoriums were popular at the turn of the century and could be found in places as varied as Martha's Vineyard Camp Meeting in Massachusetts and Chautauqua Park in Waterloo, Iowa. Publicity noted that the Junaluska auditorium was 150 feet in diameter and could seat 4,000 people.

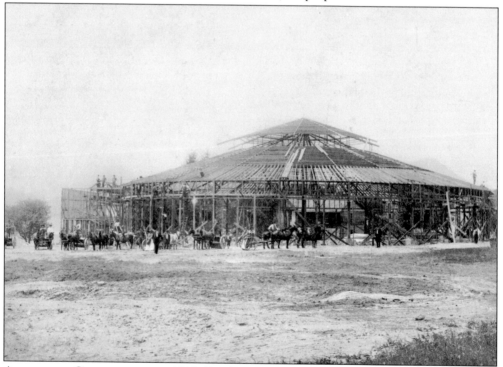

AUDITORIUM CONSTRUCTION C. 1912. Finishing touches were being applied to the auditorium as the first conference convened in June 1913. In fact, the electric lights came on dramatically during the first evening session.

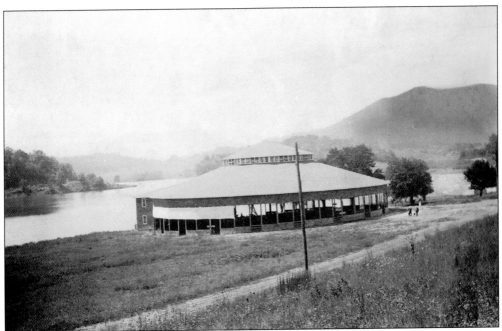

COMPLETED AUDITORIUM C. 1914. With no completed facilities other than the auditorium, participants at the first conference had to be shuttled back and forth by train to Waynesville for meals and lodging. The conference raised over $150,000 for missions, the largest amount ever in the Methodist Episcopal Church, South.

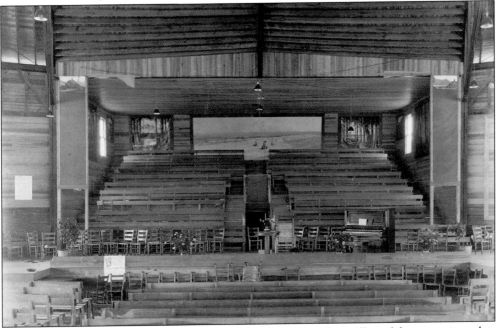

OPEN AIR AUDITORIUM. A two-story annex behind the stage floor allowed for steep risers that could presumably seat 500 people. In one of the most surprising discoveries in the photographic record, the mural facing the audience at the top of the risers was a large ocean scene complete with bathers on the beach. The heavy wooden benches do not appear to provide much comfort.

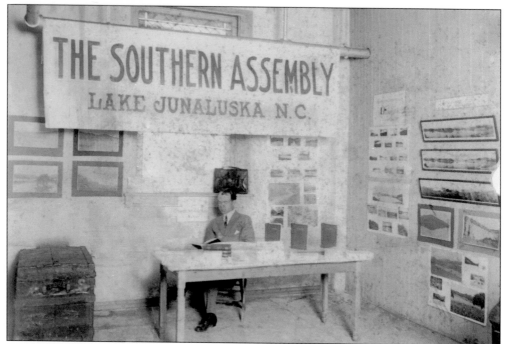

SOUTHERN ASSEMBLY. J. Dale Stentz, son-in-law of George R. Stuart, became superintendent of the assembly in 1924. This appears to be a rather sparse office where one could get an overview of the plans and development of the grounds. In 1929, the name was officially changed to the Lake Junaluska Methodist Assembly.

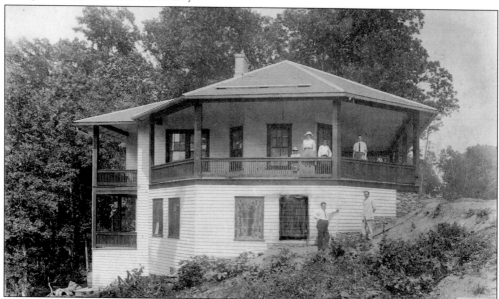

FIRST HOME. The first home on the grounds at 334 Atkins Loop was called Nyda, built by C. E. Weatherby Sr. of Faison, North Carolina. Weatherby, lay leader of the North Carolina Conference, donated the bell by the auditorium and built and ran Providence Lodge. He is pictured on the porch with his wife, Nyda, and sons Vernon, age eleven, and Carleton Jr., age four. The additional gentlemen are unidentified. (Courtesy of Jean Weatherby Edwards.)

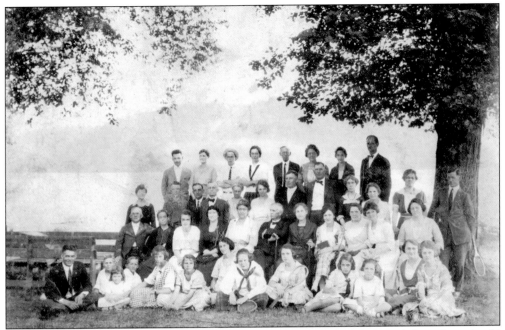

INTRODUCING LAKE JUNALUSKA. Rev. Nath Thompson, friend of Bishop Atkins, brought 44 members from his church in Norcross, Georgia, to visit the Southern Assembly. With all ages represented and tennis rackets visible, they clearly came to partake of all the assembly had to offer. Thompson is on the third row, eighth from left with the bow tie. (Courtesy of Julia O'Neil.)

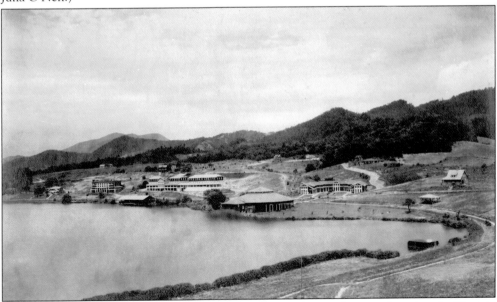

ASSEMBLY GROUNDS, 1920. This 1920 vista, facing northwest, features three hotels: Virginia Lodge at left (later called the Cherokee Hotel), the College Inn with its new annex (later named the Terrace Hotel), and the horseshoe-shaped Auditorium Hotel. The new Carolina Road winds up the hill on the right, and the long road on the crest of the hill with two houses in the distance on the left is Littleton Road.

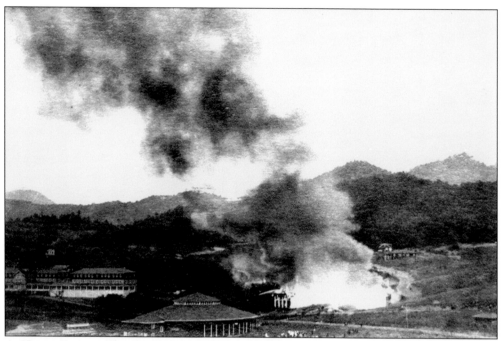

A Hotel Burns. The Auditorium Hotel—a multipurpose, centrally located building with assembly offices, a small store, rooms for guests in the summer, and a boarding school in the winter—burned in October 1920.

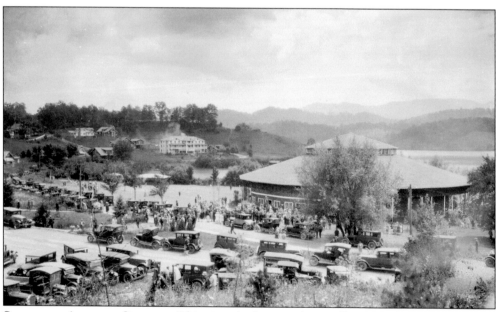

Southeast Assembly Grounds. This vista, looking southeast, illustrates the growing parking problem, the children's playground to the left of the auditorium, and the Colonial Hotel across a curve of the lake.

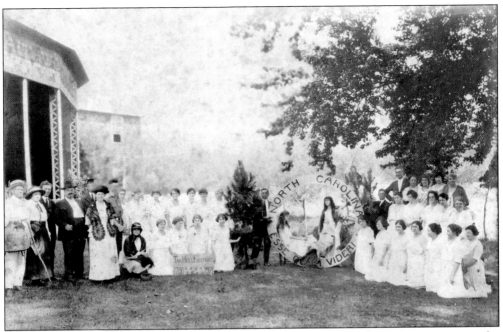

JUNALUSKA STUNT NIGHT, 1921. First-place winner in stunt night entertainment at the auditorium in 1921 was an adult group performing "Tar Heel Footprints, 1700–1921." It is difficult to guess what scenes made up the historical tableau, but the illustration of the seal of North Carolina is perfect. (Courtesy of Jean Weatherby Edwards.)

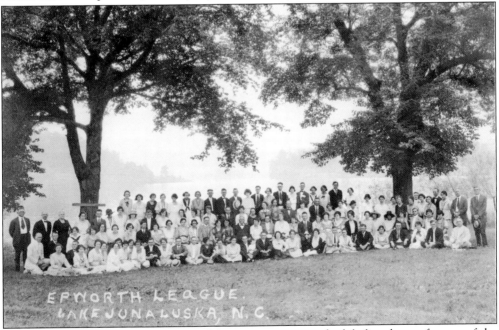

EPWORTH LEAGUE CONFERENCE, 1921. Most every summer schedule listed a conference of the Epworth League, the church's youth program. The conferences were training events for leaders of all age groups, offering inspirational addresses, Bible and mission study, supervised recreation, and instruction in the latest methods in leadership.

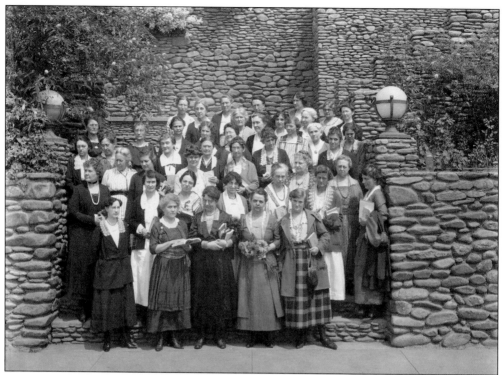

Women, 1920s. Recurring conferences for women in the 1920s were the annual meeting of the Board of Social Service and Temperance and those of the Woman's Missionary Society and the Young Women's Christian Association (YWCA).

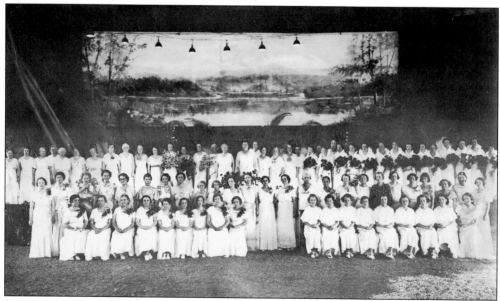

Woodmen of the World, auxiliary, 1936. This picture of a women's group of the Woodmen of the World shows that the mural of a beach scene behind the stage in the auditorium had been replaced with one of the lake. Rearrangement of the benches reveals the sawdust floor of the auditorium.

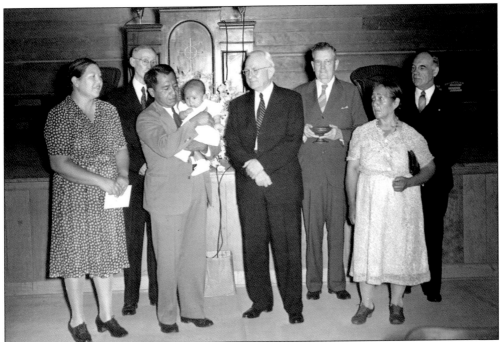

BAPTISM OF NATIVE AMERICAN BABY. For years the auditorium was the only venue for weddings and baptisms. Here Native Americans from the nearby Cherokee Indian Reservation baptize a baby in Stuart Auditorium. Forbis Durant, minister at the Cherokee Mission Church from 1942 to 1945, holds the baby, perhaps his own, with what could be his wife and a relative or friend looking on. Participants include Bishop Clare Purcell (center) and Supt. F. S. Love holding the baptismal font.

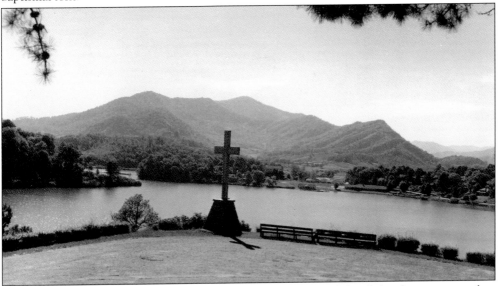

THE CROSS. The iconic symbol of Lake Junaluska Assembly is a 25-foot lighted cross mounted on a five-foot pedestal of native stone. It is situated overlooking the lake on the high point of North Lakeshore Drive. The location also perfectly frames the cross against the unique formation of Junaluska Mountain.

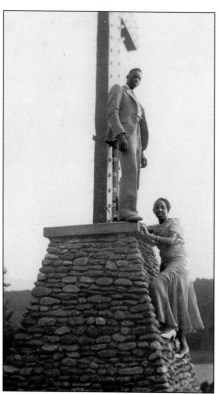

VISITORS AT THE CROSS. These visitors in the 1920s cannot resist having their picture taken at the cross. This photograph is from an album of snapshots with no identification or date that was mailed to the Heritage Center.

CLOSE UP OF CROSS. The pose of an unidentified group before the cross illustrates its original construction. The cross was replaced in 1994 with a slightly different pattern of light bulbs.

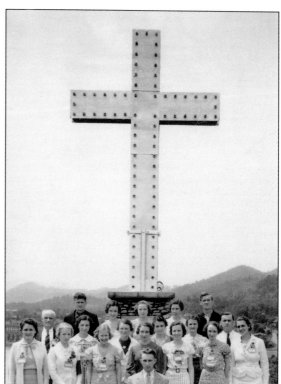

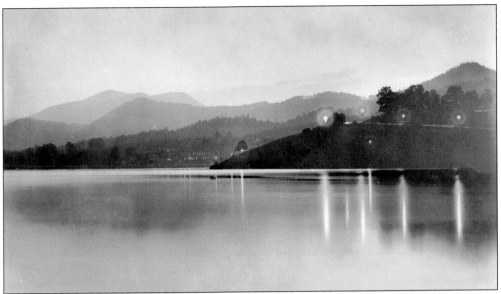

NIGHTTIME VIEW OF THE CROSS. The cross was a gift of the Federation of Wesley Bible Classes of the Western North Carolina Conference in 1922. At the end of the summer season, the electric cross was turned off, only to have engineers on the nearby railroad request that it remain lit for their enjoyment and inspiration. The cross has remained lit all year ever since.

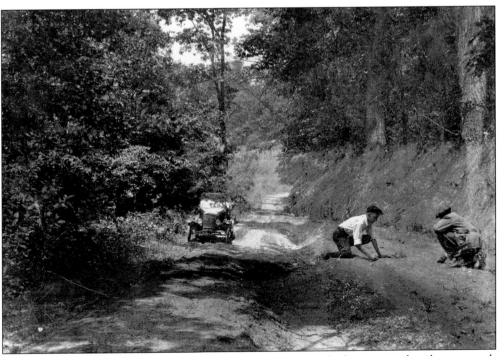

AN EARLY MOUNTAIN ROAD. Resort areas in the mountains had to contend with poor roads despite the growing popularity of automotive travel. A promotional booklet in 1912 boasted of 75 miles of good roads in the area connecting nearby towns with the assembly. A "good road" could turn quite muddy quickly.

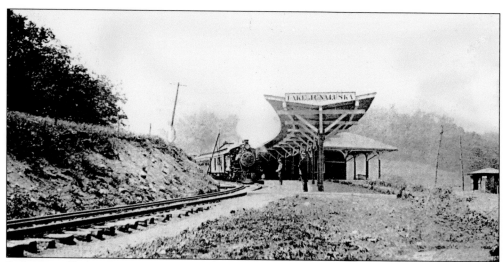

JUNALUSKA TRAIN STATION. The Southern Assembly was purposely located on a railroad line, and most of the early travelers arrived by train, often taking advantage of special promotions. One cottage owner remarked that nothing was more pleasant than leaving the heat of the lowlands behind and arriving overnight by train in the beautiful, cool mountains.

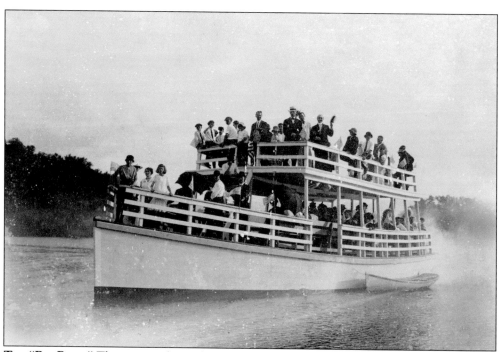

THE "BIG BOAT." This picture shows the maiden voyage of the Big Boat. Originally named *The Oonagusta* after Chief Junaluska's wife, it was later simply called the *Cherokee*. It was christened by "Tib" Stuart, daughter of George R. Stuart, in 1914. (Courtesy of Jean Weatherby Edwards.)

CAPTAIN WESCOTT. Capt. J. T. Wescott ran the *Cherokee* for many years. The *Cherokee* was a working boat, hauling passengers and baggage from the train station across the lake for 10¢ one way. There was no bridge across the dam until 1920. (Courtesy of Lucy Aldridge Hinson.)

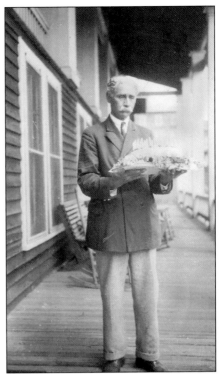

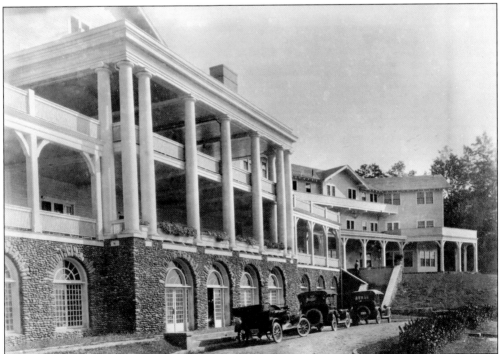

THE JUNALUSKA INN. "The Pride of the Lake," the Junaluska Inn opened on the hill above the dam in 1917. Tragically the hotel burned to the ground July 10, 1918, after less than two years use. World War I raging in Europe also affected the 1918 season.

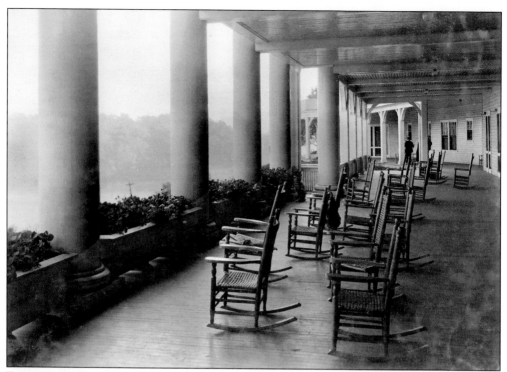

PORCH OF THE JUNALUSKA INN. Rocking chairs and a wide porch invite relaxation, contemplation, or friendly conversation, staples of the Junaluska experience.

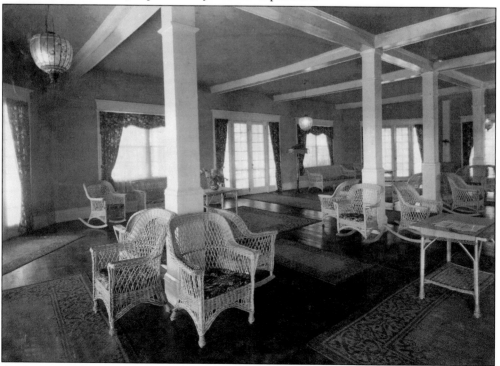

AN INTERIOR VIEW OF THE JUNALUSKA INN. Here is the elegant interior lobby of the inn.

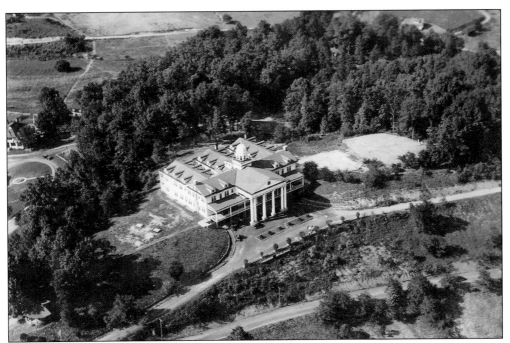

MISSION INN AERIAL VIEW, 1922. The Mission Inn, which replaced the Junaluska Inn, was originally named with the intent of being a place where missionaries could stay while on furlough and was later named for Bishop Walter R. Lambuth, a prominent missionary and church leader. Lambuth Inn became a primary hotel because of the earlier loss of two large hotels by fire.

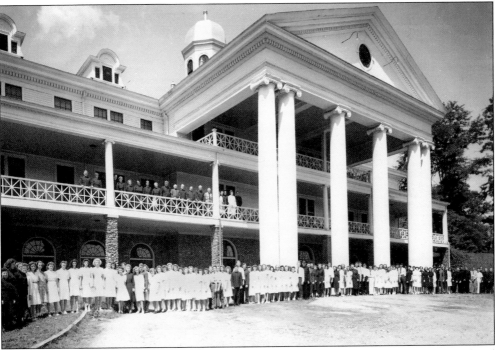

LAMBUTH INN. With everyone in some sort of service uniform, this unidentified, undated photograph appears to include the complete staff of the inn.

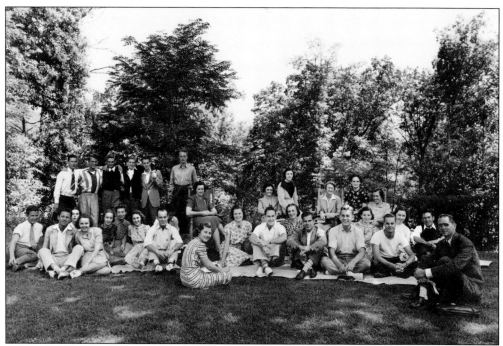

DUKE UNIVERSITY SUMMER SCHOOLS. Professor Mason Crum (right) poses with the students of his Religion and the Family course outside Lambuth Inn in 1938. Duke University operated a summer school directed toward certification for schoolteachers (1926–1939) and a school of religion for interested pastors and laymen (1928–1941) on the assembly grounds. (Courtesy of Mason Crum papers, Duke University Archives.)

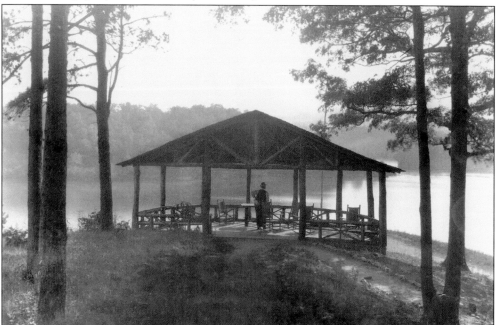

INSPIRATION POINT. Inspiration Point, located near Lambuth Inn above the cross, originally had a covered structure for enjoyment in all kinds of weather.

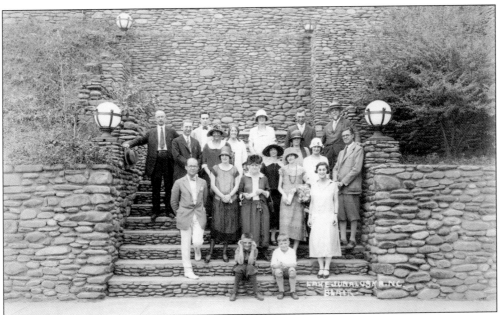

TERRACE HOTEL STEPS. An unidentified group photographed on the steps of the Terrace Hotel in the 1920s has some assembly leaders. Bishop James Cannon Jr. (fourth row, left) was the first superintendent of the assembly. John R. Pepper (fourth row, right) was president of the board of trustees. J. Dale Stentz (second row, left) was superintendent of the assembly and active in the music program.

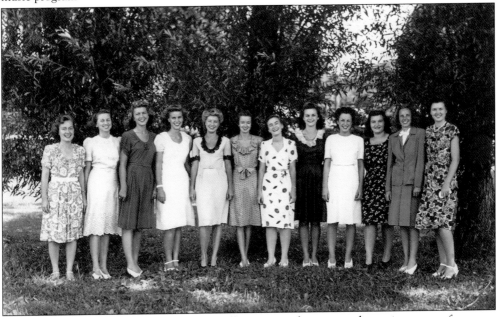

TERRACE HOTEL SUMMER STAFF, 1944. College-age students were the main source of summer staff at the Terrance Hotel. The 1944 summer staff included, from left to right, Betty Chreitzburg, Skeeter Morris, Kit and Mary Crum, Carolyn Broome, Betsy Perry, Skippy Herbert, Pat Crum, Rose McDermot, Peggy Herbert, Dot Durdin, and Betsy Cade. Dr. Mason Crum and his wife, Catherine, managed the Terrace that summer. (Courtesy of Betty Chreitzburg Crenshaw.)

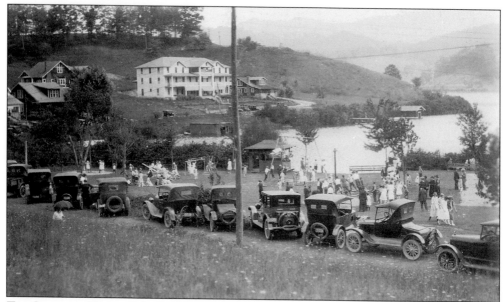

THE COLONIAL HOTEL. T. L. McClees, a contractor in Durham, North Carolina, discovered the assembly as a summer vacation retreat and investment. He built the Colonial Hotel in 1922, securing the summer session of a boys' school in Florida as a sure tenant. Sisters Nellie McClees and Bertha McClees Aldridge later operated the hotel for years. The assembly purchased the Colonial and renovated it in 1971.

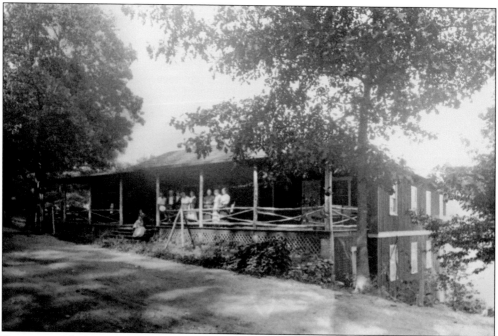

PROVIDENCE LODGE, C. 1920. With the major hotel fires, smaller private accommodations for guests were welcome alternatives. Providence Lodge, built in 1913 on Atkins Loop, is still in operation. Rooms rented for $2 per day in 1917.

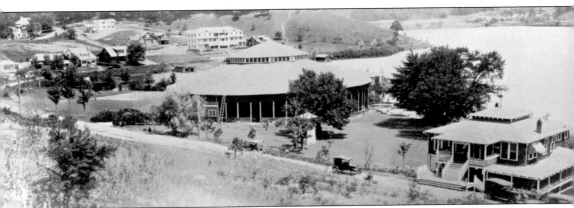

THE ADMINISTRATION BUILDING. This vista includes the first administration building (right), which was located next to the auditorium by the lake. It had assembly offices on the first floor and the popular soda shop and a camera shop downstairs.

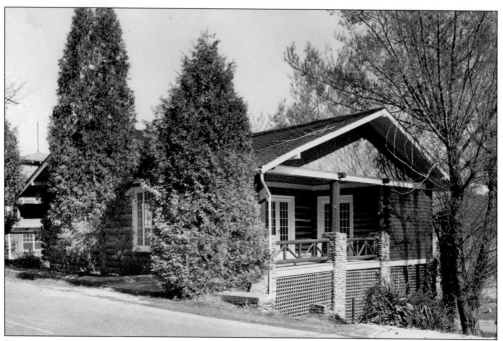

THE BOOKSTORE. The original Cokesbury Bookstore, built in 1925, was an inviting log building beside the lake next to the administration building. It was later moved to nearby Burghard Circle, now called Cokesbury Circle, and converted to a residence.

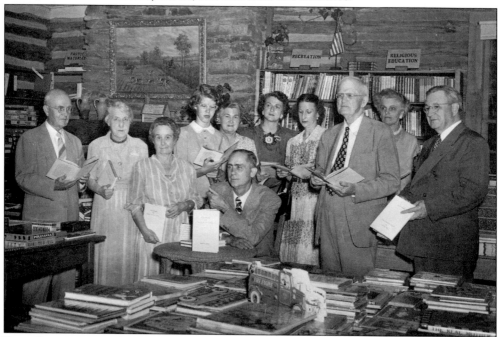

BOOK SIGNING, 1950. Dr. Mason Crum (seated) autographs his book *The Story of Lake Junaluska* in the bookstore in 1950. Looking on are, from left to right, Dr. J. M. Ormond, Mrs. D. M. Litaker, Katrina Ormond, Mary Moore, Mrs. Barber, Mrs. Gramling, unidentified, J. B. Ivey, Mrs. O. M. Litaker, and Dr. W. F. Quillian.

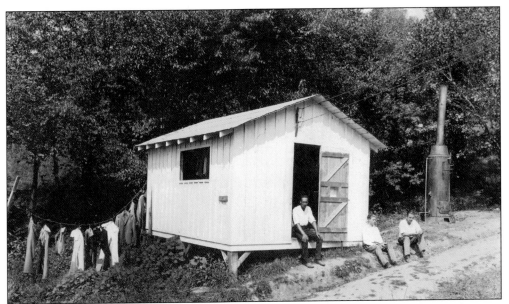

DRY-CLEANING BUSINESS. J. F. Dusenbury (seated in the middle) operated a dry-cleaning business on the grounds. It was located along hotel row on North Lakeshore Drive where the Susanna Wesley Garden is at present.

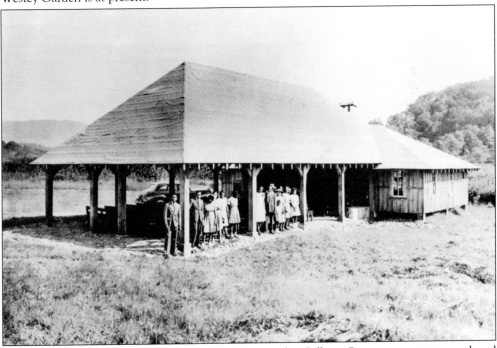

THE GILBERT CENTER. Located near the cafeteria, the Gilbert Center was constructed and opened in 1941. It was a gathering and worship place for African American staff and servants brought to the assembly by cottage owners. The Gilbert Center was dismantled when the Jones Cafeteria was built, and a room in Lambuth Inn was dedicated to Gilbert in 1980. The assembly went through a long and contentious path to eliminate segregation, forced in part by some church agencies refusing to meet at Junaluska until it was fully integrated.

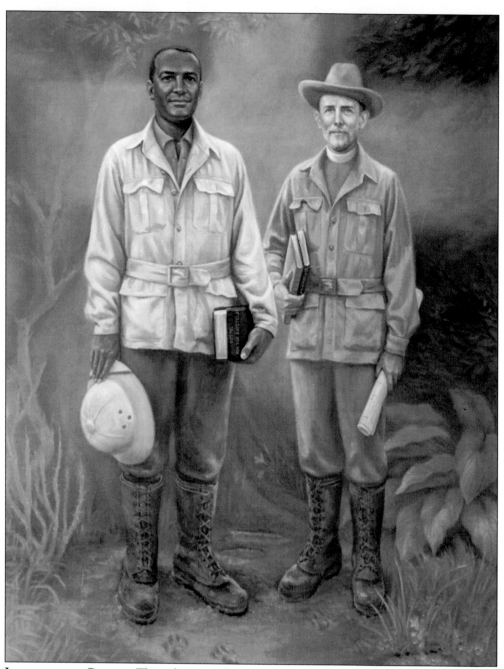

LAMBUTH AND GILBERT. This oil portrait hangs in the Gilbert-Lambuth Memorial Chapel at Paine College in Augusta, Georgia. It depicts John Wesley Gilbert (left) and Bishop Walter R. Lambuth as they embark on a missionary journey to Africa in 1911. Gilbert, a native of Georgia, was a minister, accomplished linguist, and professor at Paine College. Lambuth, born in China to missionary parents, became a missionary physician and minister, founding hospitals and schools in China. The Gilbert Center and Lambuth Inn were named for these two influential Methodists. (Courtesy of the artist, Anna Evelyn Barnes.)

Two

THE DREAM EXPANDS

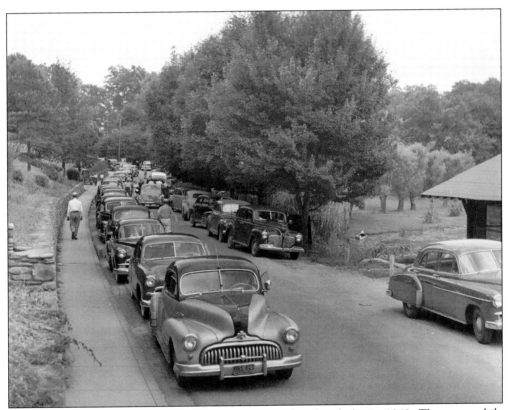

POSTWAR CHANGES. The last passenger train stopped at Junaluska in 1949. The automobile culture in America had been steadily building in the 20th century, but the Great Depression and pervasive attention to winning World War II slowed family driving and even halted the production of automobiles. Pent-up consumer demand burst forth in the late 1940s. More conferees and residents arrived at Junaluska by car—many the newest models. Problems with narrow roads and demands for parking became readily apparent. Increasing prosperity also increased the desire for newer facilities. Lake Junaluska Assembly was on the way to being rebuilt.

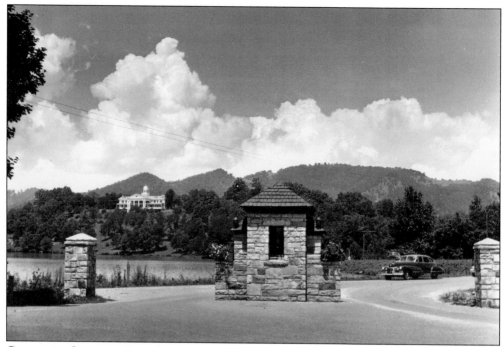

GATES AND GROUNDS FEE. The stone east gate, the gift of Mrs. K. J. Day of Kentucky, opened near the dam in 1939, and a west gate was added in 1948. Gate boys were employed to welcome visitors, answer questions, give directions, and collect grounds fees.

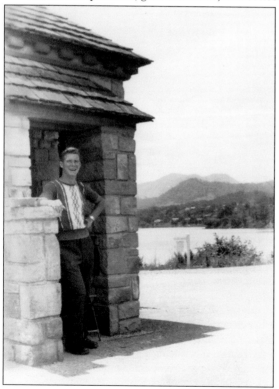

SUMMER EMPLOYMENT. Arthur M. "Art" O'Neil, a student at Millsaps College, applied for a summer job in 1951 and was offered one as a gate boy. He traveled to Junaluska overnight by bus, never having been to the mountains before, and found a place to stay free at Providence Lodge in exchange for doing yard work. O'Neil worked as a lifeguard the next few summers. Later, as a Methodist minister, he bought a home on the grounds. His experience was not atypical. (Courtesy of Julia O'Neil.)

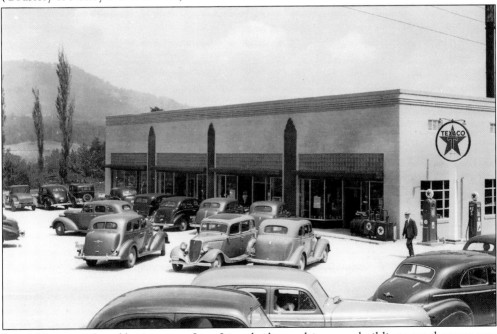

GROUNDS FEE. The stone gates gave increased focus to the collection of a grounds fee to defray maintenance costs and help underwrite assembly programs. In 1950, rates varied from one-half day for 30¢, $2.25 for a week, and up to $7.50 for a season's pass. Cottage owners, children, staff, and servants paid varied reduced rates. The state-maintained County Road to the back of the assembly grounds was a gaping hole in the system, but the fee remained in effect until 1967. (Courtesy of Nancy Hobbs Banks.)

LINER BUILDING. Local businessman Jerry Liner built a multipurpose building near the west gate in 1940, where one could buy groceries, household and hardware items, and visit the post office. Liner is an unsung hero of Junaluska. When the assembly had to declare bankruptcy in 1932, he was named temporary receiver, thus keeping the operation going until better times.

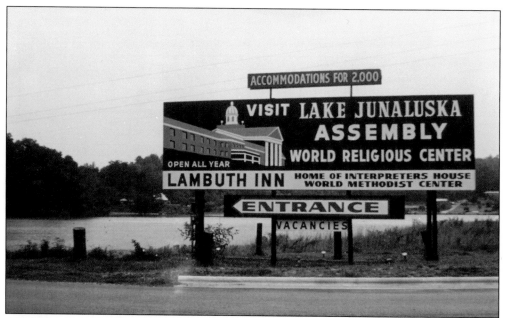

AN APPEAL AT THE NEW WEST ENTRANCE. The bypass of Waynesville, which passed by the upper end of the lake, was completed in 1948. This new road presented another opportunity to advertise assembly facilities. After a portion of the lake was filled in, a new entrance gate and road were built in 1977. The assembly officially adopted year-round operation in 1984.

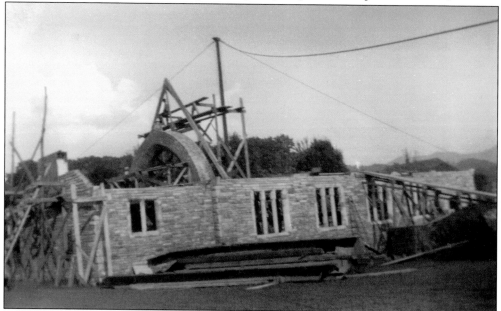

CHAPEL CONSTRUCTION. In 1944, the Cottage Owners Association campaigned for a more intimate, worshipful space than the auditorium. The idea of a chapel won immediate support, but it was 10 years before a completed building was dedicated. Problems with fundraising, selection and acquisition of stone, design changes, and cost overages caused Guy Fulbright, one of the construction supervisors, to proclaim, "If I ever get that thing done, I'd never start nothing like that no more."

36

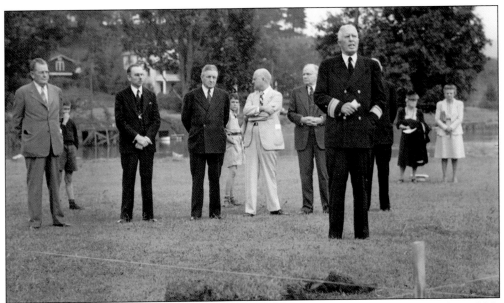

GROUND-BREAKING FOR THE CHAPEL. Rear Adm. William N. Thomas, chief of chaplains, U.S. Navy, delivers the address at the ground-breaking of the chapel in November 1946. From left to right, Supt. F. S. Love, C. C. Norton, W. F. Quillian, Elmer T. Clark, and Bishop Costen J. Harrell participate in the service. The chapel is used year-round, seats 280, and is a popular place for weddings.

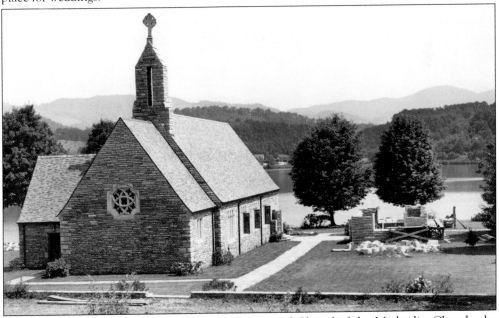

THE MEMORIAL WING. Officially named the Memorial Chapel of the Methodist Church, the chapel is a memorial in honor of southern Methodists who served in the armed forces during World War II. Each church in the jurisdiction was asked to send the names of its service personnel and $1 for each one memorialized, thus raising approximately $60,000 of the $100,000 cost of the building. The Room of Memory to be connected to the chapel is under construction on the right.

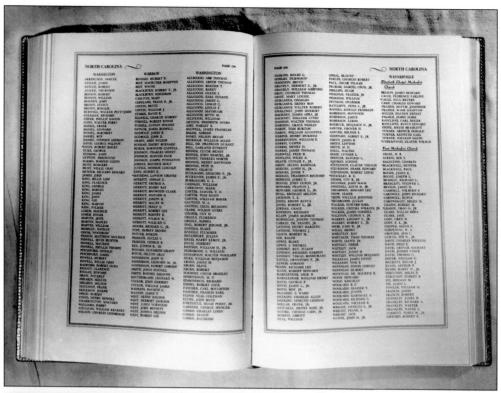

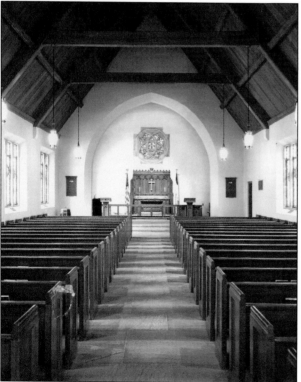

THE MEMORIAL BOOK. The Memorial Book lists the names of 90,000 men and women. That number is not the total of those who served in the military from the ecclesiastical geographic area represented, as some churches did not participate in the solicitation.

INTERIOR OF THE CHAPEL. Charles W. Brockwell's booklet, "The Memorial Chapel: An Appreciation," aptly describes the detail of the Gothic chapel topped with a Celtic cross. The stained glass windows were designed by Elmer T. Clark and Bishop Costen J. Harrell, with six of the eight given by annual conferences of the Southeast Jurisdiction of the Methodist Church.

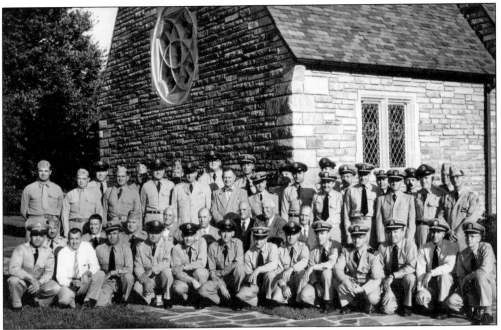

CHAPLAIN'S RETREAT, 1952. Between 1941 and 1946, the Methodist Church sent 1,747 men into the military chaplaincy—486 of them from the southeast. Some 28 Methodist chaplains died in World War II, 13 of whom were from the southeast jurisdiction.

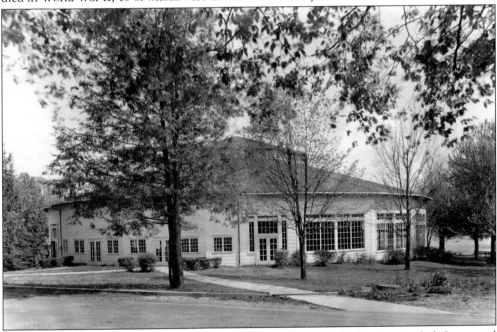

THE AUDITORIUM CHANGES. Much needed changes to Stuart Auditorium included a partial concrete floor and theater seats in 1942 and an assembly room and classroom addition behind the stage in 1945. The new Hart Memorial Sound System dealt with a perennial problem in 1969, and the first heating system in 1986 contributed to year-round operation. (Courtesy of the *Mountaineer*.)

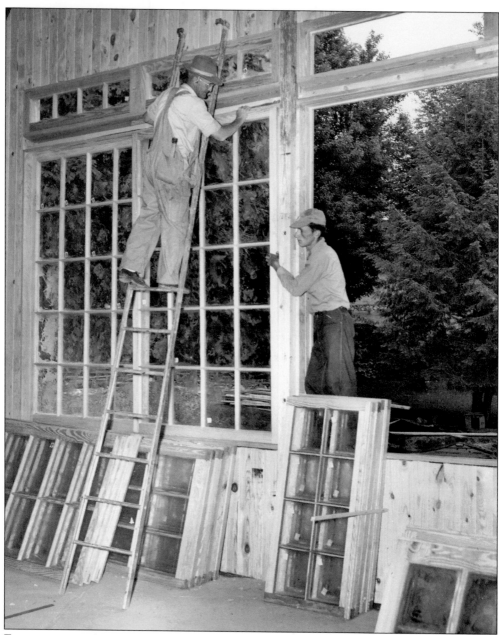

ENCLOSING THE AUDITORIUM, 1951. T. M. Kuykendall and Sely Rhodarmer install windows, enclosing the auditorium. Mason Crum, a renowned storyteller, maintained that it was necessary to complete the concrete floor in 1951 due to wandering dogs that carried fleas that lived in the sawdust floor. Parents lost a babysitting aid when boys could no longer play with toy trucks in the sawdust during services. Birds and dogs were eliminated as a distraction, although dogs occasionally wandering on the stage added to the entertainment.

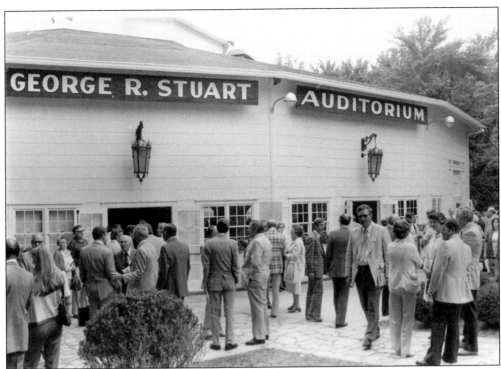

GEORGE R. STUART AUDITORIUM. In addition to many outstanding preachers, the auditorium hosted famous speakers over the years: William Jennings Bryan in 1916, Madam Chiang Kai-shek in the late 1930s, Eleanor Roosevelt in 1944, Vice Pres. Richard M. Nixon in 1955, NBC television anchorman Chet Huntley in 1967, and Georgia governor (and later U.S. president) Jimmy Carter in 1973.

SPECIAL EVENTS. William K. Quick (left), chair of the planning commission, and Bishop Paul Hardin hold commemorative medals honoring the bicentennial of the arrival of Francis Asbury in America in 1771. Asbury, the circuit-riding bishop who directed the growth of the Methodist Church to the largest denomination in the new nation, probably traversed Junaluska grounds on a trip in November 1810. (Courtesy of the *Mountaineer*.)

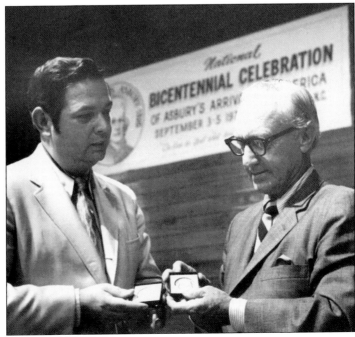

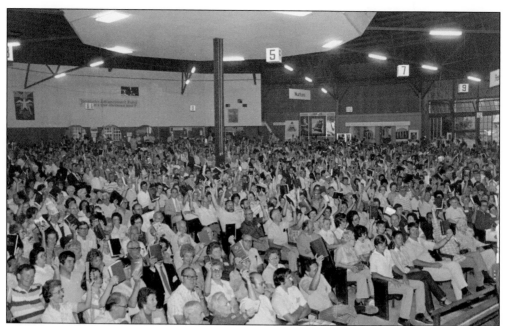

A Full House. Stuart Auditorium has had its share of outstanding preaching. George R. Stuart was tremendously popular in the early decades. Later churchmen of renown were Kagawa from Japan, William Sangster and Reginald Mallett from England, and Americans Ralph Sockman, Wallace Hamilton, and Gerald Kennedy.

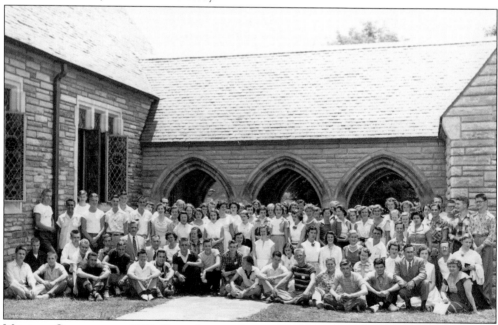

Missions Conference, 1952. From the very first event in 1913, conferences on missions were among the largest in attendance. Speakers from around the world were featured, and each conference had an adult and youth division. Here are youth attending from throughout the jurisdiction in 1952. Many attendees were making their first visit to Junaluska and many entered full-time Christian service. (Courtesy of Norwood Montgomery.)

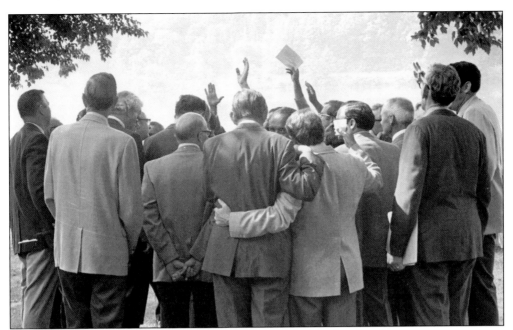

A Meeting Place. Many caucuses have met beside the lake deciding how to vote on an issue before a governing conference. Junaluska became the permanent meeting place of the quadrennial Jurisdictional Conference in 1956, and the site of the annual meetings of the Western North Conference in 1957 and the Holston Conference in 1978. (Courtesy of the *Mountaineer*.)

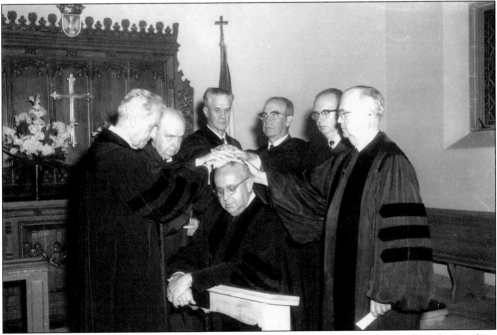

Consecration of Bishop Goodson. W. Kenneth Goodson of the Western North Carolina Conference was elected bishop in 1964. Assisting in his consecration are, from left to right, Bishop Nolan B. Harmon, Bishop Costen J. Harrell, A. Glen Lackey, Frank B. Jordan, Charles D. White, and Bishop Paul N. Garber.

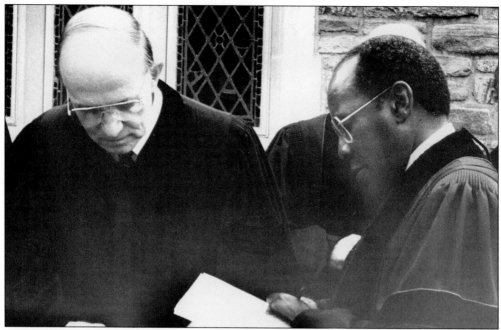

BISHOP BETHEA. H. Hasbrouck Hughes Jr. of Virginia (left) and Joseph B. Bethea were elected bishops in 1988. Bethea, the third African American bishop to serve and the second elected in the southeastern jurisdiction, had served the church in various capacities in Virginia and the Carolinas, and had been director of black church studies at the Duke Divinity School. A new welcome center at Junaluska was named for Joseph B. and Shirley C. Bethea in 2007.

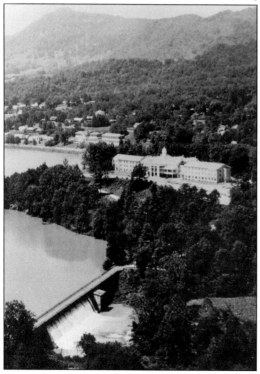

EXPANDED LAMBUTH INN. Lambuth Inn more than doubled in size with the opening of a west wing in 1956 and an east wing in 1964.

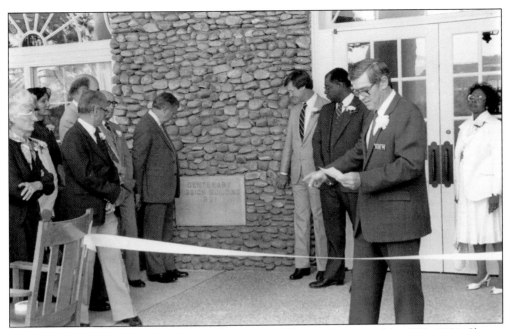

REOPENING OF LAMBUTH INN. The last renovation of Lambuth occurred in 1983–1984. Shown at the opening after the modernization are, from left to right, Hilda Harbin, unidentified, Jeff Reece, R. Wright Spears, Clay Madison, Robert Ralls, Joe Hale, William Morris, Mel Harbin and Mary Morris.

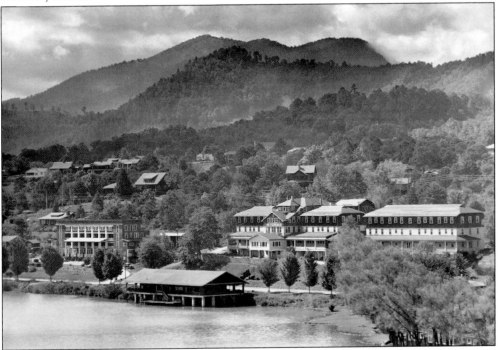

LAST LOOK AT THE ORIGINAL LAKEFRONT. This familiar vista was soon to give way to a much needed modern hotel, a new all purpose building, and facilities for two new programs with headquarters on the grounds.

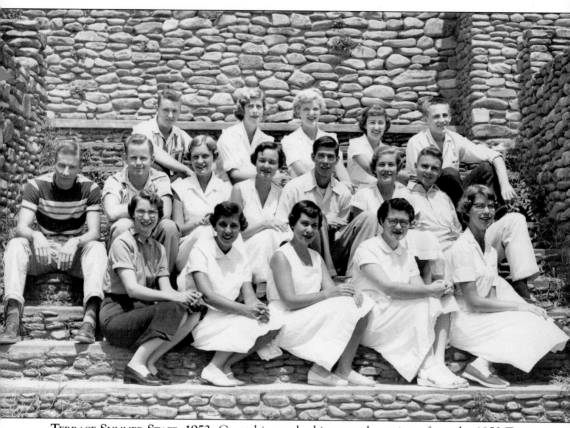

TERRACE SUMMER STAFF, 1953. Courtship resulted in several marriages from the 1953 Terrace summer staff. The staff included, from left to right, (first row) Ruth Smith, Pat Lineberger, Cathryn Buck, Mary Berry, and Mary Moore; (second row) Woody Adams, Jim Thurman and future wife Edith Bridges, Pat Lanius and future husband Henry Bynum, Joy Brantley, and Harry Beverly; (third row) Jan Westmoreland, Ellie Mitchell, Peggy Sherffey, Ann Wiley, and Charlie Haygood. Mary Moore married Jimmy Hamilton, and Woody Adams married Lucy Neely. (Courtesy of Jim Thurman.)

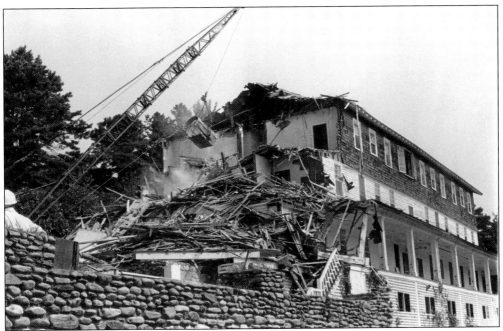

AN ORIGINAL MAINSTAY REPLACED. The original rambling Terrace Hotel made way for a more modern facility with demolition in 1973.

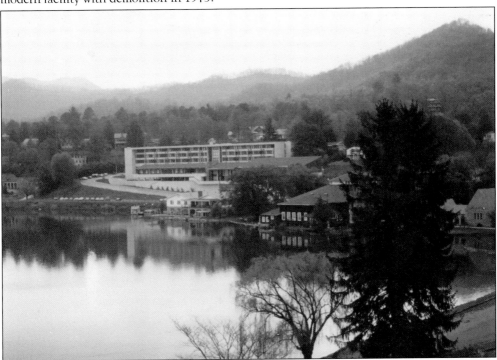

THE NEW TERRACE HOTEL. The new Terrace Hotel was built in two phases beginning in 1974. Phase one, which opened in 1977, consisted of guest rooms and a temporary lobby. Phase two was completed in 1979 and added the lobby, dining room, a 300-seat auditorium, meeting rooms, and a large lounge with a fireplace.

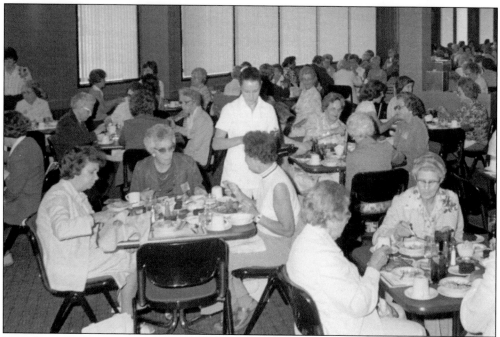

NEW TERRACE DINING HALL. The new dining hall and kitchen had the capacity to serve 330 people. The United Methodist Women of the South Carolina Conference were the first visitors served in May 1979.

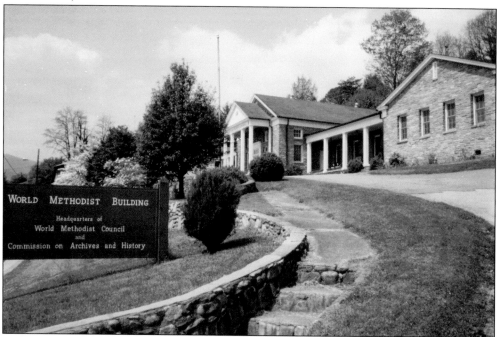

WORLD METHODIST BUILDING. The headquarters of the World Methodist Council was built on the site of the original Cherokee Hotel in 1955. The newly created General Commission on Archives and History of the Methodist Church shared the building in 1968 but later relocated to Drew University in 1978.

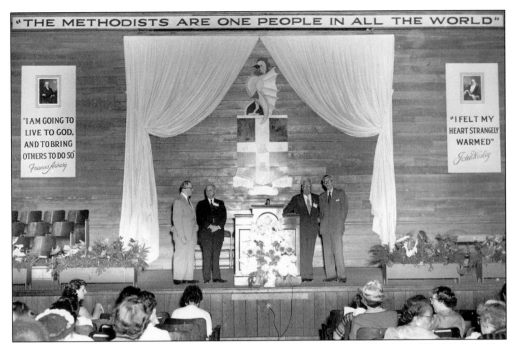

NINTH WORLD METHODIST CONFERENCE. Stuart Auditorium set up for the Ninth World Methodist Conference in 1956. Over 70 organizations that share the Methodist/Wesleyan heritage in over 130 nations work together through the World Methodist Council. Founded in 1881, its headquarters was relocated to Junaluska in 1956. (Courtesy of the World Methodist Museum.)

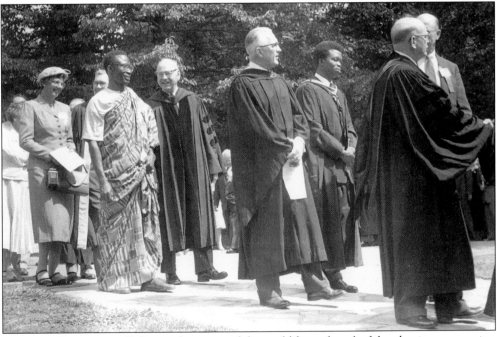

ACADEMIC PROCESSION. Delegates from around the world formed a colorful and unique procession at the Ninth World Methodist Conference in Stuart Auditorium. The conference convenes every five years at different locations around the world. (Courtesy of the World Methodist Museum.)

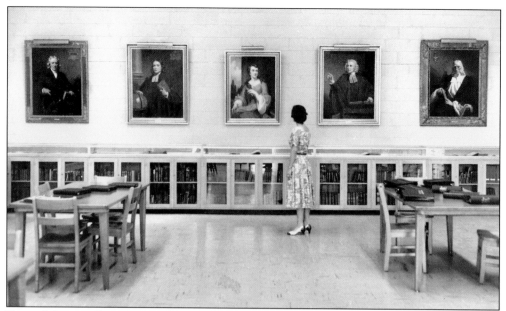

EARLY MUSEUM DISPLAY. A photograph of an early configuration in the World Methodist Museum features portraits of the founders of Methodism by artist Frank O. Salisbury. The portraits are, from left to right, of Francis Asbury, Thomas Coke, Susanna Wesley, Charles Wesley and John Wesley. (Courtesy of the World Methodist Museum.)

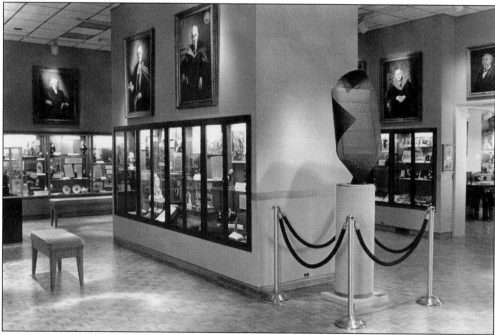

RENOVATION AND AN EXPANDED MUSEUM, C. 1983. The World Methodist Museum, located in the original World Methodist Building, is the largest collection of Methodist historical artifacts and memorabilia in the United States. Of particular interest is the original portable pulpit founder John Wesley carried about when preaching in the open fields in England. (Courtesy of the World Methodist Museum.)

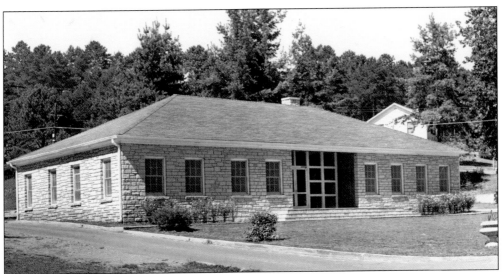

A New Administration Building. A much needed administration building was built across from Stuart Auditorium in 1952 and named for H. G. Allen, a former superintendent. It was renamed in 1975 when the name of Bishop John W. Branscomb was removed from the craft building and it became the Allen-Branscomb Administration Building. It was enlarged in 1975 and again in 1989.

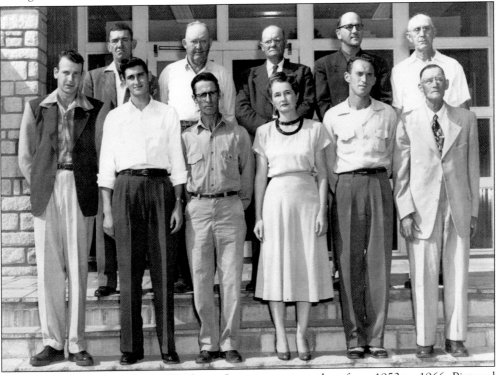

Administrative Staff. James W. Flower Jr. was superintendent from 1953 to 1966. Pictured here from left to right is the assembly staff early in his tenure: (first row), two unidentified, Jack Finney, Ila Campbell, Lewis Jones, and unidentified; (second row) Jack Frizzell, unidentified, Millard Gaddis, Jim Fowler, and Sam Gaddis. (Courtesy of Margaret Fowler McCleskey.)

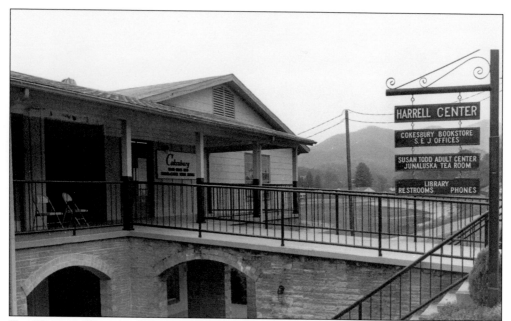

THE HARRELL CENTER, 1960. The old, unheated multipurpose boathouse was replaced in 1960 by a modern building named for Bishop Costen J. Harrell. It contained an adult center, tearoom, and library as in the older building and a new bookstore and added offices for the jurisdiction staff. (Courtesy of the *Mountaineer*.)

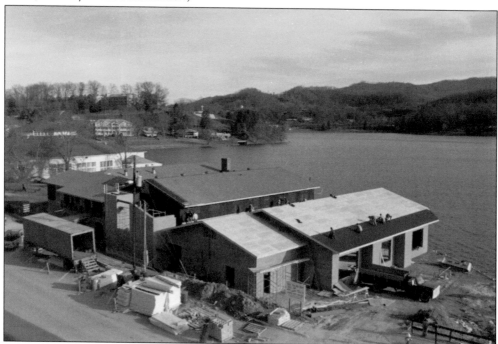

AN EXPANDED HARRELL CENTER. The Harrell Center was renovated and enlarged in 1988 to include a 500-seat auditorium as the assembly moved to more year-round programming. The Southeastern Jurisdiction Heritage Center, which moved from Nashville, Tennessee, to the Liner Warehouse in 1983, moved to the Harrell Center in 1989.

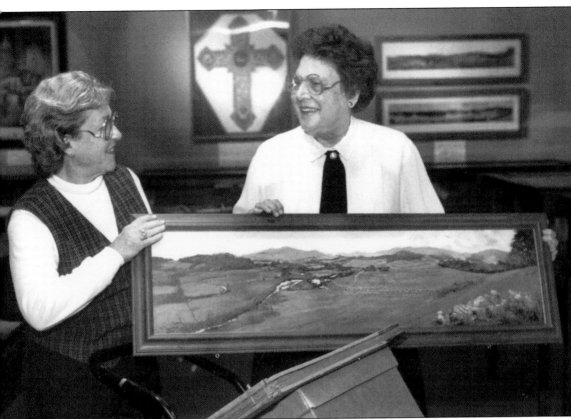

STALWARTS IN PRESERVING HISTORY. Frances Cobb Hart (left), as director of the Heritage Center from 1987 to 1992, and Daisey Holler Wilson, as an indefatigable collector, are the two individuals most responsible for preserving the history of the assembly. Hart planned and carried out the move of the Heritage Center to the new modern facility. Wilson donated her large collection of historical materials to the repository. Each developed a special affection and loyalty to the assembly as second-generation residents who raised their own families at the lake. (Courtesy of Melford A.Wilson.)

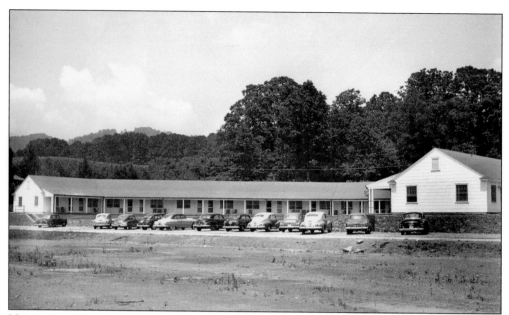

NEW-STYLE ACCOMMODATIONS. The first apartment-style accommodation opened in 1949, coinciding with the end of passenger train service. Additional apartments opened in 1951 and 1952, forming a complex near the west entrance. The assembly provided another living option when Tri-Vista Condominiums were completed in 1986.

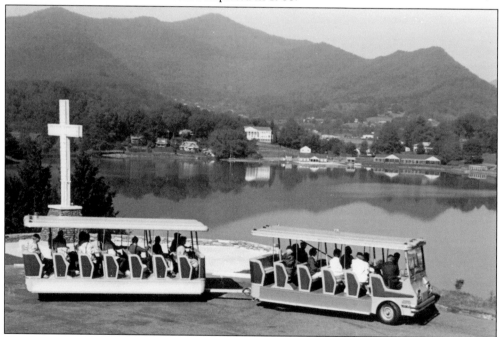

THE JUNALUSKA ASSOCIATES. A major financial support group, the Junaluska Associates, was formed in 1968. Membership was $100 a year. The Junaluska Associates have contributed over $3.3 million for the beautification of the grounds and support for program. One of the first improvements was the purchase of a trolley to transport guests about the grounds. (Courtesy of the Intentional Growth Center.)

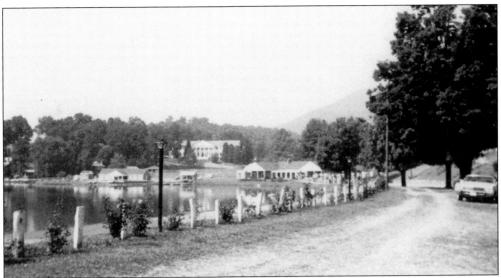

THE ROSE WALK. In 1962, Lee F. Tuttle, executive secretary of the World Methodist Council, planted a few roses along the walk by the lake in front of the headquarters building. This modest beginning became the much admired, greatly expanded row of around 125 rose bushes, featuring approximately 35 varieties. The Junaluska Associates provide annual financial support for the purchase of plants and materials, and half the salary of the horticulturist who cares for the grounds.

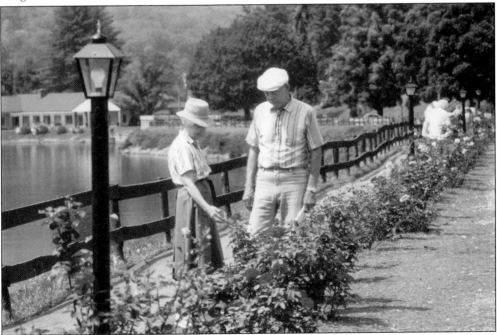

THE ROSE WALK EXPANDS. The popularity of the Rose Walk and the need for parking and safety along the lakeside path necessitated improvements. Part of the lake had been filled in to provide for perpendicular parking, and now a fence was needed between the path and the lake. This led to the gradual construction of a paved walking path around the entire lake, financed by major gifts of donors and the Junaluska Associates.

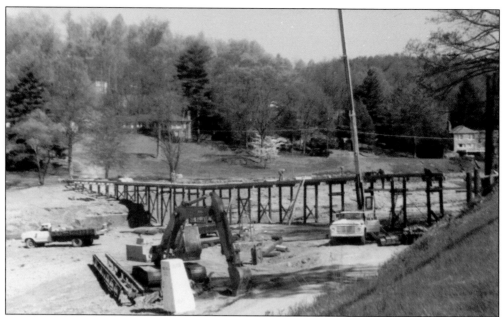

THE LAKE NARROWS BRIDGED. There was talk of a bridge across the narrows that divided the lake into two distinct parts in 1913, but the project was not a priority. Additional unfunded plans included the generation of electricity at the dam for a trolley line around the lake. Spurred on by the interest of the Junaluska Associates, a couple came forth to fund the walking bridge in 1988.

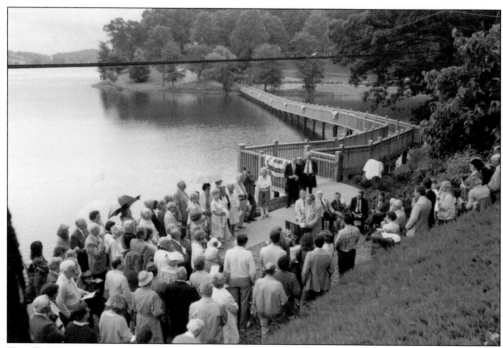

THE TURBEVILLE BRIDGE. Donors Paul M. and Willie May Turbeville of Bradenton Florida were honored at the dedication of the Turveville Bridge in 1988. One end of the bridge was raised to permit the tour boat, *Cherokee IV*, to pass underneath.

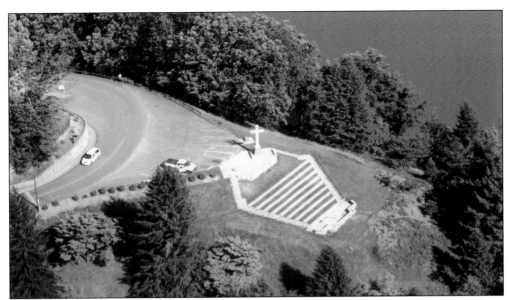

AMPHITHEATER AT THE CROSS. Youth groups have been hiking to the cross from their facilities at the west end of the grounds for years. The Junaluska Associates funded the construction of an amphitheater for outdoor services at the site in 1988. It is the location of an annual Easter sunrise service and a popular site for weddings. (Courtesy of the Junaluska Associates.)

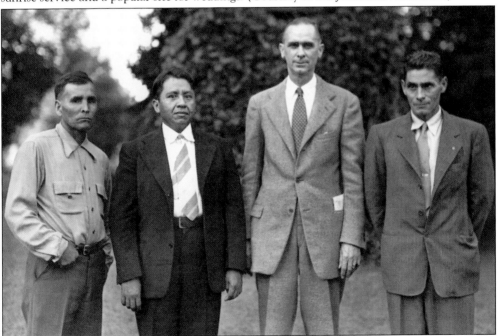

LECTURE ON JUNALUSKA. The lake, assembly grounds, and nearby mountain overlooking the lake are named for Junaluska, a revered leader, frequently called chief, of the Cherokees who reside in the area. Mason Crum presented a public lecture on Junaluska in the mid-1940s. In attendance were, from left to right, Moses Owl; Rev. Forbis Durant, direct descendant of Junaluska; Mason Crum, minister at the Cherokee Methodist Mission Church; and Chief Jarett Blythe, head of affairs at the nearby Cherokee reservation.

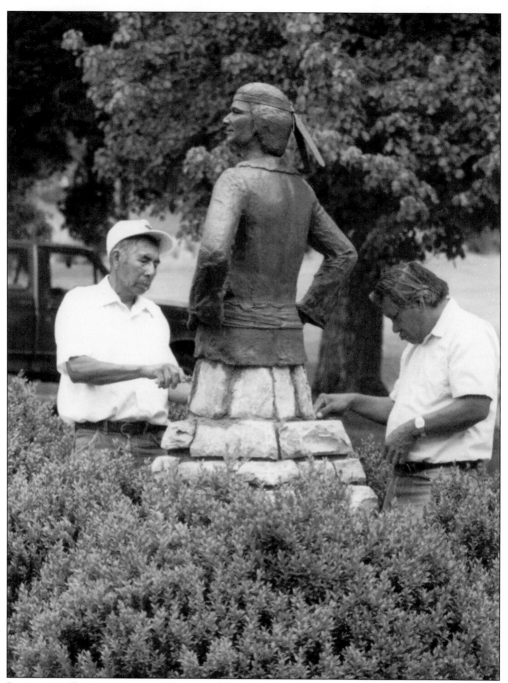

JUNALUSKA COMMEMORATED. The assembly erected a bust commemorating Junaluska outside Stuart Auditorium in 1988. The Junaluska Associates also honor Junaluska with the Chief Junaluska Award, given for meritorious service to Lake Junaluska and the United Methodist Church. In 1814, Junaluska saved the life of Andrew Jackson in the Creek Indian War. When Jackson was president, Junaluska visited him, imploring him not to remove the Cherokees from their native land. His plea failed, and most of the tribe was forced to walk to the new Indian Territory in Oklahoma in 1838, a journey that became known as the Trail of Tears.

Three

A Focus on Christian Education

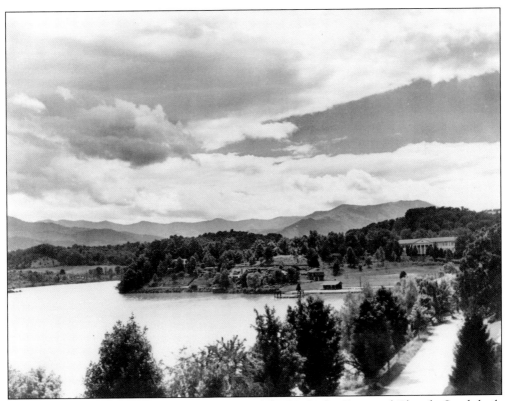

A New Focal Point. The board of education of the Methodist Episcopal Church, South built a religious education building at Junaluska in 1923. Its primary purpose was to be a training center for Christian education. The Christian education movement was similar to campaigns in public education focusing on proper learning techniques, teacher training, and curriculum development. It also moved the church away from narrow fundamentalism. The large building on a hill at the west end of the lake is a prominent focal point for the assembly grounds.

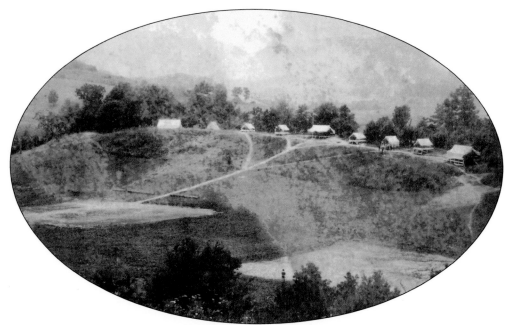

ACCOMMODATIONS BEFORE HOTELS. Early accounts refer to guests and residents camping in tents before permanent buildings were erected. A rare photograph from 1916 illustrates a row of tents on the hill later occupied by the board of education building. The tents are either for conference attendees or for campers at Camp Eureka. (Courtesy of Martha Gay Duncan.)

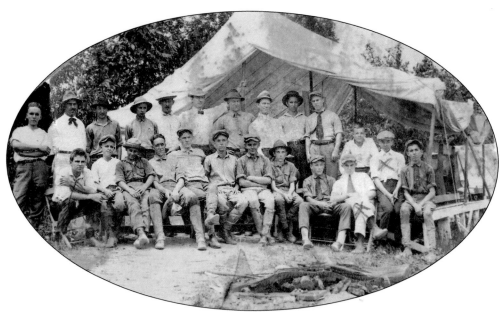

TENT CAMPING. The Epworth League Conference of 1914 advertised tents as an alternative to more expensive hotels. In the likely event of rain or mud, conferees or campers at least had raised wooden floors for their tents. (Courtesy of Martha Gay Duncan.)

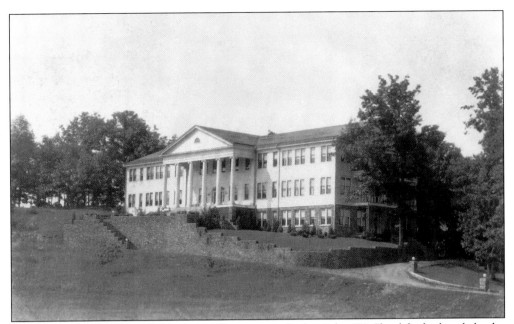

SHACKFORD HALL. The education building is named after John W. Shackford, church leader in the developing Christian education movement. He founded the adult Wesley Bible class movement and led the plan to create a single general education board by merging three boards in 1930. (Courtesy of Lucille Bellamy.)

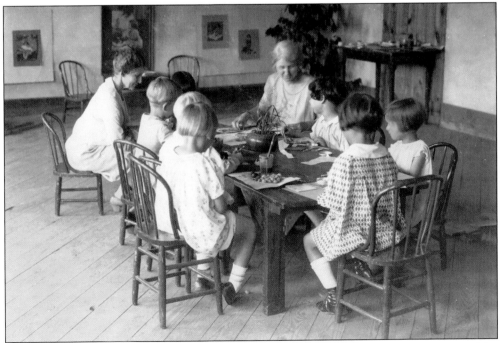

CLASSROOM INSTRUCTION. Mounting debt for the assembly in the 1920s put program opportunities in a bind. The interior of Shackford Hall was not completely finished until the 1950s.

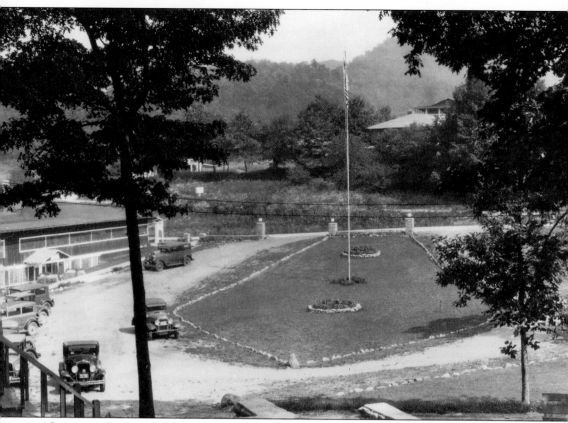

INVITING GROUNDS. With the educational program a major focus of the assembly, inviting grounds and permanent buildings were developed at the west end of the grounds to house and feed numerous annual conferences for all ages.

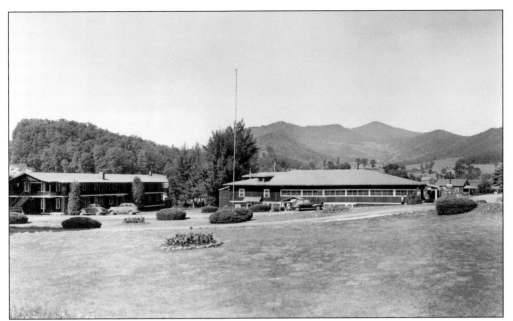

DORMITORIES AND A CAFETERIA. The Sunnyside Lodge (left), Sunday school cafeteria (right), and an additional dormitory called Mountainview Lodge all were built in the 1920s for the Christian education campus.

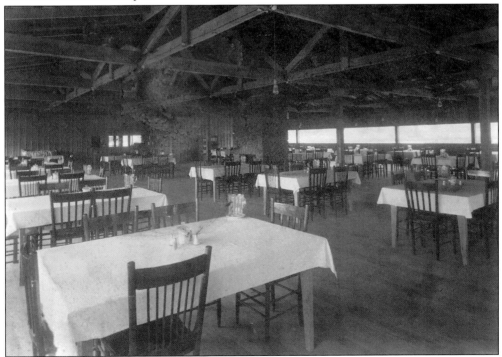

INTERIOR OF THE CAFETERIA. Dining together was an integral part of the Christian education experience. Life in the mountains and recreational activities increased one's appetite, and fellowship with new friends and group singing added to the joy of attending conferences at Junaluska.

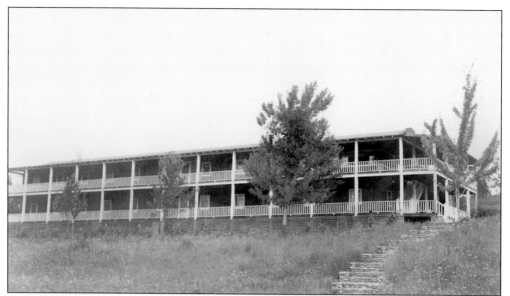

UPPER LAKESIDE LODGE. In 1922, J. B. Ivey built the Lower and Upper Lakeside Lodges, matching buildings with a separate kitchen in between. The lodges served as overflow for conferences in Shackford Hall and as a less expensive place than hotels for young families with children to stay. The assembly later purchased the buildings, demolished them, and built a new Lakeside Lodge in 1985.

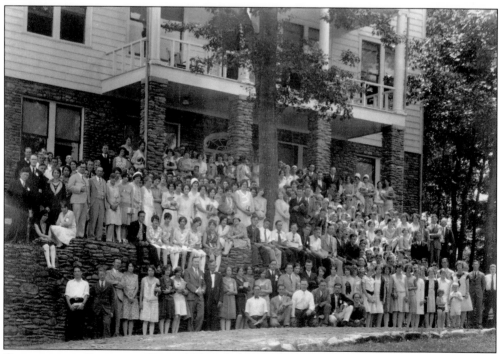

CONFERENCE IN SHACKFORD HALL. Although this photograph is unidentified, annual conferences in Shackford in the 1920s included both jurisdictional and Western North Carolina Conference Epworth League meetings, a Young People's Conference, and Sunday School Conference of the General Sunday School Board.

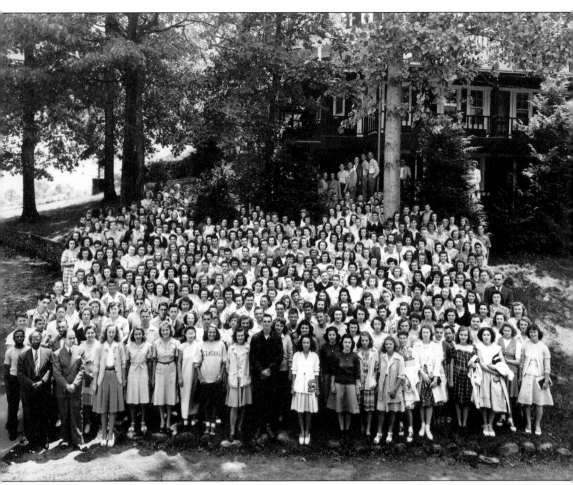

YOUTH CONFERENCE, 1944. The Western North Carolina Conference had an annual training conference for Methodist youth fellowship leaders from the mid 1930s to 1980. This is an impressive gathering in 1944 given wartime restrictions. Mountainview Lodge is in the immediate background with Shackford Hall barely visible behind it.

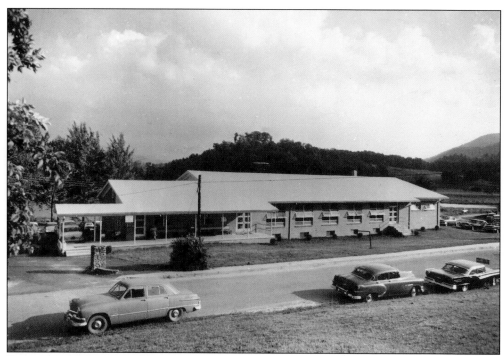

EDUCATIONAL GROUNDS REBUILT. A new cafeteria named for Edwin L. Jones, a businessman from Charlotte, North Carolina, was built in 1958. As chairman of the board of trustees from 1948 to 1968, Jones presided over much of the planning and rebuilding of the grounds.

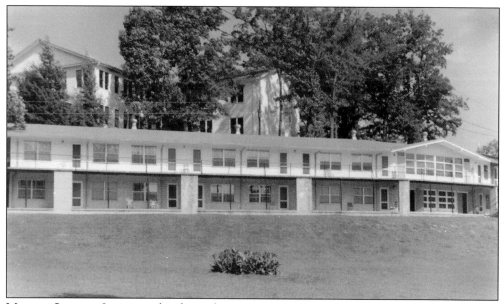

MODERN LODGES. Long overdue for replacement, a new Mountainview Lodge and Sunnyside Lodge were built in 1957 and 1958. Sunnyside was relocated around the hill behind Shackford Hall.

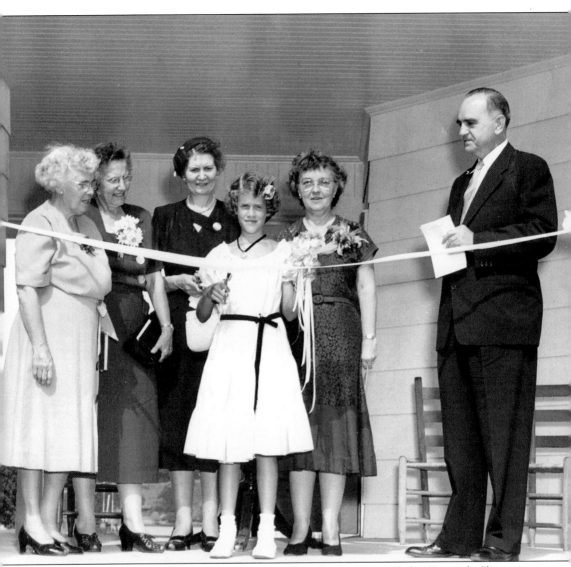

CHILDREN'S BUILDING OPENING, 1953. Presiding at the opening of the Kennedy-Skinner Children's Building in 1953 are, from left to right, Mrs. Christian Rauschenberg (Lina), vice chair of the building committee; Edith Willis Reed, first director of children's activities; Ruby Sandefur, former secretary to Mary Skinner; Margaret Owen, grandniece of Skinner; Elizabeth Jarrett, chair of the building committee; and Dr. Carl H. King, treasurer of the building committee. (Courtesy of the Kennedy-Skinner-King Children's Building, Wilson Children's Complex.)

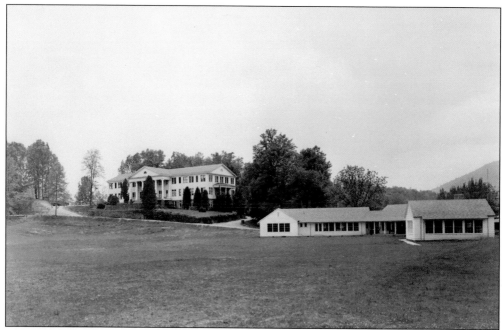

NEW FACILITY FOR CHILDREN. The Kennedy-Skinner Children's Building near Shackford Hall opened in 1953. It was named for Minnie E. Kennedy and Mary E. Skinner, influential educators in the general education board. An addition in 1968 was named in honor of Dr. Carl H. King, Junaluska trustee and head of the educational program of the Western North Carolina Conference from 1934 to 1967.

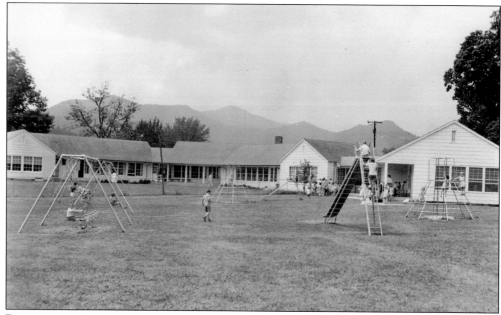

PLAYGROUND RELOCATED. First moved from next to Stuart Auditorium to the vicinity of the swimming pool, the J. B. Ivey Playground was relocated near the new children's building in 1954. Initially Carl H. King supervised planting shade trees, adding new play equipment, and hiring professional and summer staff for the expanded program of children's activities.

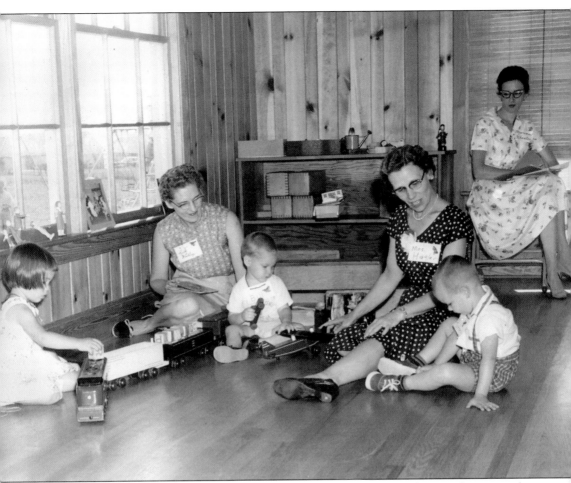

LABORATORY SCHOOL. Annual leadership and laboratory schools brought educators from around the country to instruct teachers in Christian education in the newest professional concepts and methods. Educators taught while classes of adults observed and then discussed the methods and experience afterward.

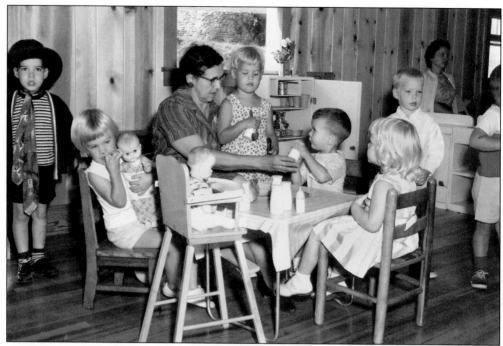

A Preschool Class. The lab schools focused on proper stages of development and the introduction and best methods to teach age-appropriate curriculum. Children of Junaluska residents and staff served as pupils in the lab schools.

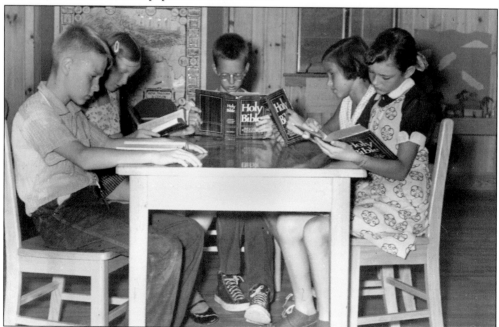

A Teenage Class. Lab schools certified teachers in appropriate instruction from preschool to adult education. The Christian education emphasis brought the Sunday school, vacation Bible school, Epworth League, and later Methodist Youth Fellowship experience in line with best practices in the public and private schools.

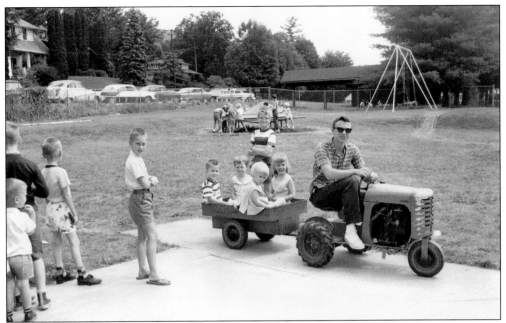

TRACTOR RIDE. Summer employee Johnny Holt begins the popular tractor ride around the playground. The craft shop and nature study were also popular, as well as Fun 'N Frolic on Wednesday nights, which featured a bag supper and free play until the lightning bugs came out and it was time to go home.

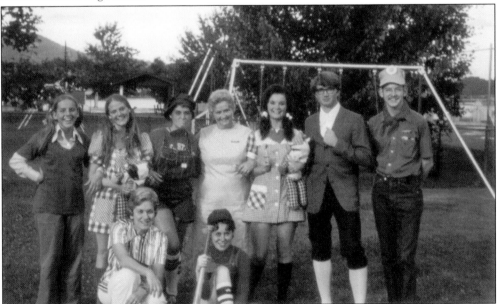

STORYBOOK NIGHT, 1973. Storybook night in the 1970s was part of a fully staffed children's program. The playground was open seven days a week with a Sunday schedule of Sunday school for children and parents and two story hours in the afternoon. Summer staff in 1973 were, from left to right, (first row) Peggy Ormond and Mary Rogers; (second row) Grier Fields, Susan Anderson, Terri Tucker, Mary Follis (director), Joanna Paul, unidentified, and George Lashley. (Courtesy of Mary Rogers Garrison.)

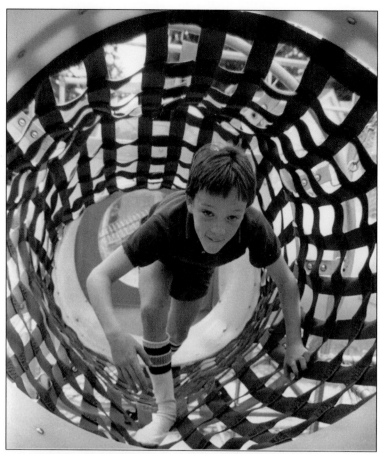

MODERN PLAY EQUIPMENT. Modern play equipment was added to the Ivey Playground in 1985. On the left, 10-year-old Mark Gilbert climbs in some new apparatus, and the bin of balls below looks like so much fun adults dive in, including Supt. Mel B. Harbin at right. (Left, courtesy of the *Mountaineer*.)

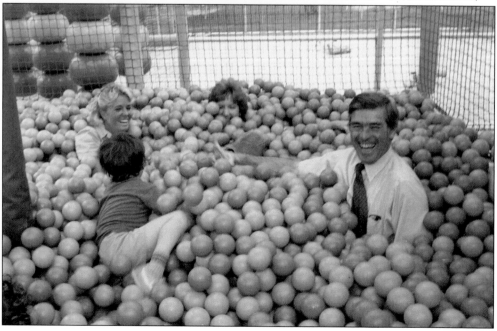

Four

A TRADITION OF MUSIC

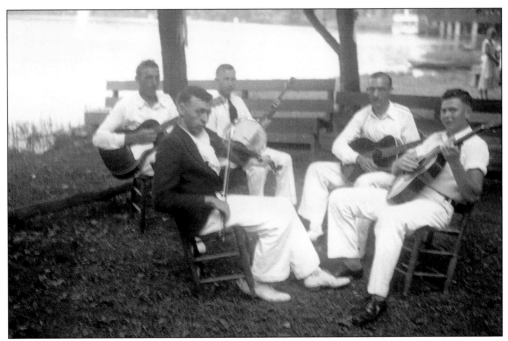

LOCAL MUSICIANS ENTERTAIN. A variety of music, both in worship and entertainment as well as musical instruction, has been part of the Junaluska experience. In the Chautauqua tradition, performances have included soloists, operettas, symphonies, and folk music—both local and international. The area has a rich tradition and variety of native talent and even sent a square dance team to the White House to perform for the King and Queen of England on the first visit of English royalty to the United States at the invitation of Eleanor Roosevelt in 1939. Here five local musicians perform by the lake at a Duke Day picnic in 1933. Methodist colleges from throughout the jurisdiction advertised themselves and attracted alumni at annual summer events. The largest program emphasizing local talent was an annual Haywood County Day, complete with singing by local church choirs, a picnic on the grounds, and a prominent speaker. (Courtesy of the Duke University Archives.)

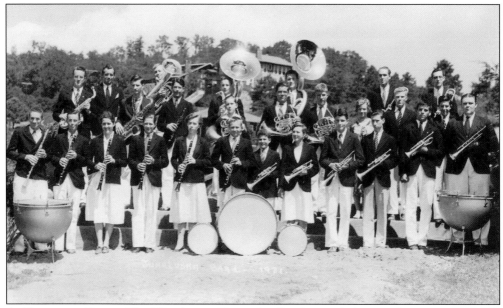

A KENTUCKY BAND. The Winchester Kentucky Band provided musical entertainment in 1930. In addition to musical performances, Stuart Auditorium hosted travelogues, lectures, spelling matches, and even silent motion pictures before "talkies" arrived. (Courtesy of Melford A. Wilson.)

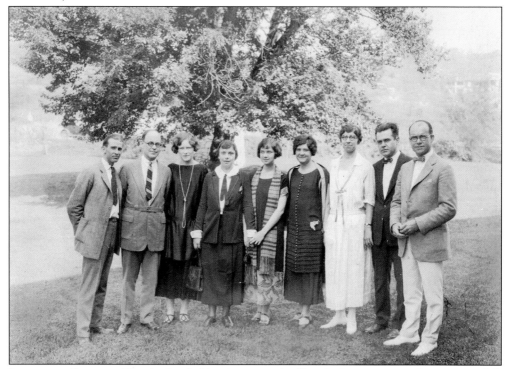

JUNALUSKA SINGERS. The back of this picture reads, "Junaluska singers in the twenties." J. Dale Stentz (right) became superintendent of the assembly in 1924 and was very active in the music program.

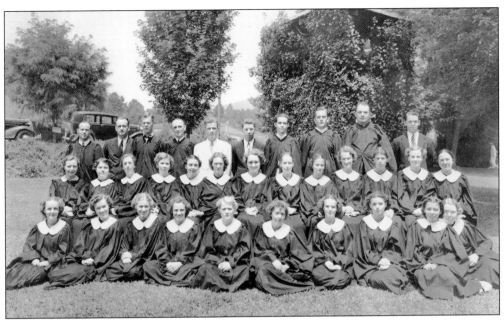

JUNALUSKA SUMMER CHOIR. Walter Vasser (third row, fifth from left) from the voice department of Greensboro College in Greensboro, North Carolina, directed the Junaluska Summer Choir in 1938 and 1939.

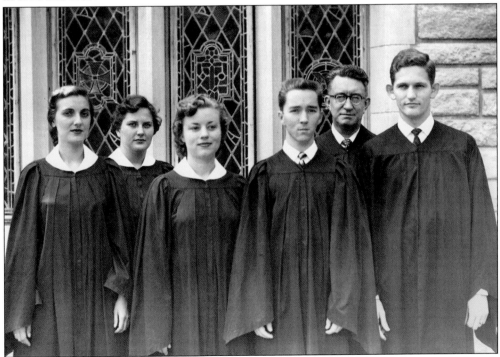

JUNALUSKA QUARTET. A paid quartet sang at assembly and conference events in 1956, with Cyrus Daniel of Vanderbilt University as director of music. The music staff consisted, from left to right, of Eugenia Toole, assistant organist; Laura Ann Harris; Charlotte Stuart; Beaman Griffin; Daniel; and Willard DeLara. A large volunteer choir sang at Sunday worship.

75

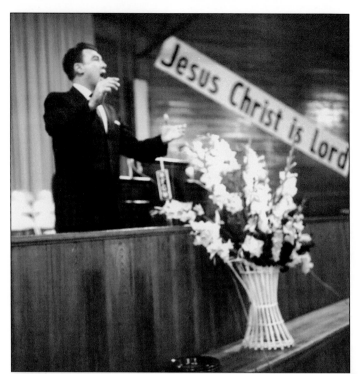

GLENN DRAPER.
Glenn Draper first came to Junaluska in 1954 as director of the Keesler Air Force Base Chorus to participate in the dedication of the Memorial Chapel. After bringing the Keesler Chorus back for popular concerts, Draper was asked to become music director at Junaluska in 1956, a position he held through 2009. He repeatedly has stated that he considers music his Christian calling.

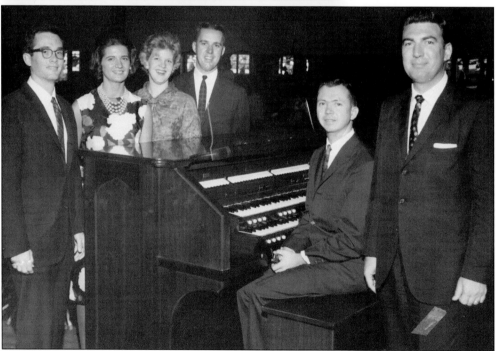

A QUARTET. The Junaluska Singers remained a quartet, with the singers of 1962 being invited to return in 1963. They were, from left to right, Michael Best, Gene Wilson, Peggy McLarty, Frank Calhoun, Euell Belcher (organist), and Glenn Draper (director). Michael Best had a successful international concert career, culminating with the Metropolitan Opera in New York City.

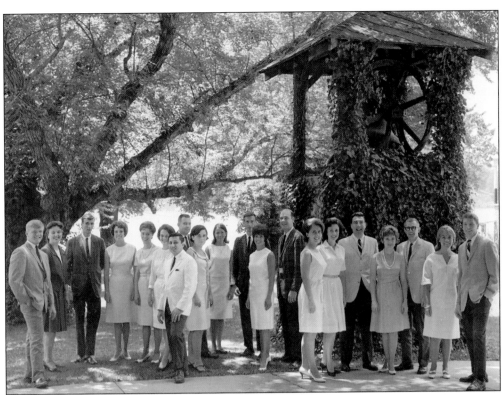

A Music Program Evolves.
The Junaluska Singers developed
a varied repertoire of sacred and
secular music, which required
additional voices. Members from
the Sunday volunteer choir
and talented residents were
recruited for an increasing number
of special concerts.

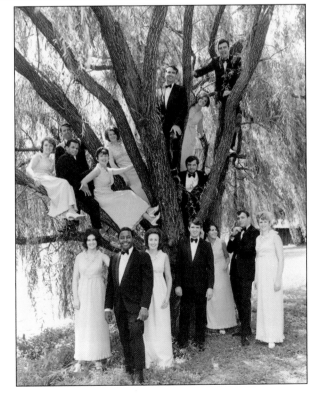

Junaluska Singers, 1969. In
1967, Draper persuaded Supt.
J. Manning Potts to replace a
Summer Artist Series with a core
group of 12 paid professional
singers. The change was made
with more faith than money, but it
proved successful, with an increase
in quality, variety, and number
of concerts.

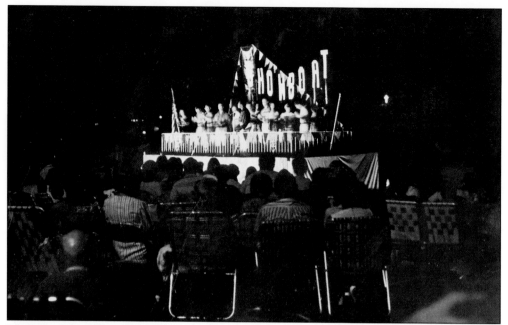

JUNALUSKA SINGERS, 1972. The *Cherokee III* provides the stage for a concert. The Junaluska Singers began touring in the United States in 1971, eventually giving concerts in England, Panama, Costa Rica, and the Holy Land.

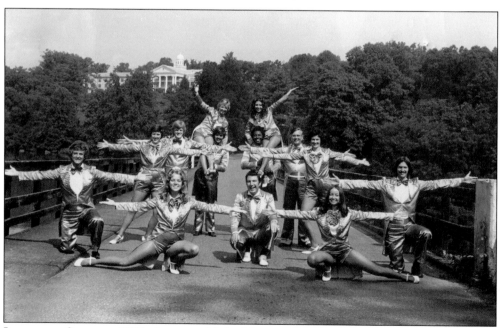

JUNALUSKA SINGERS, 1975. An annual July 4th concert preceding the fireworks display and the bicentennial celebration in 1976 provided a venue for the popular recurring A Salute to America concert series. Other themes have included "Christmas in August" and "Goin' Country." (Courtesy of the *Mountaineer*.)

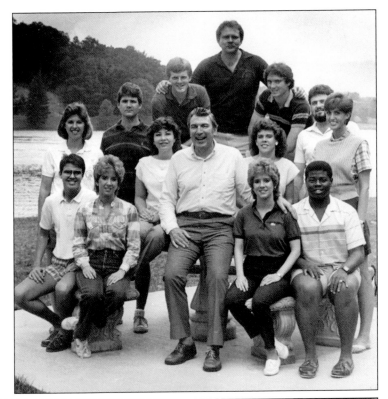

JUNALUSKA SINGERS, 1985. The Junaluska Singers are a hardworking group that has to learn fast, be alert, and "keep the energy flowing" to satisfy their director. One member noted that he learned how to change costumes 14 times in one program. Draper also emphasized that the members "get a lot at Junaluska you can't spend . . .You can't spend friends, can't spend memories, can't spend educational growth." (Courtesy of the *Mountaineer*.)

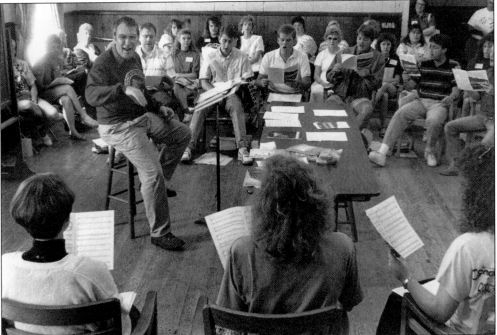

JUNALUSKA SINGERS REHEARSAL. Draper conducted the Junaluska Singers in numerous television appearances and 35 recordings. *Because of Easter*, released as both an album and a television special, was filmed while on tour in the Holy Land.

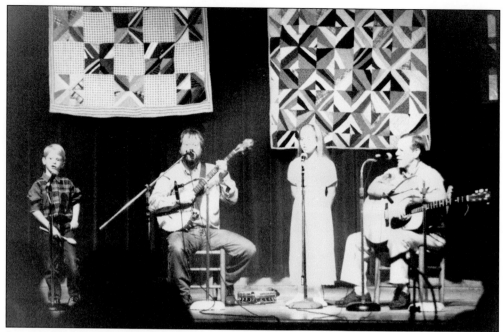

SMOKY MOUNTAIN FOLK FESTIVAL. The Smokey Mountain Folk Festival, begun in 1970, has been a popular fixture in Stuart Auditorium on Labor Day weekend for most of its tenure. Joe Sam Queen, creator and host, features a variety of local talent, such as the Trantham family, pictured here. (Courtesy of Joe Sam Queen.)

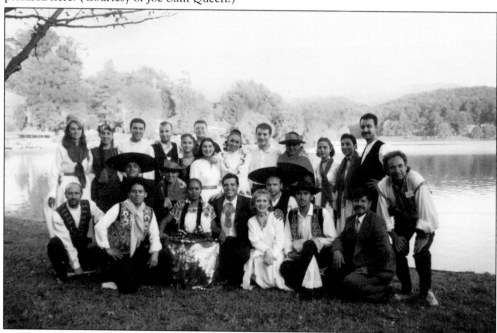

FOLKMOOT AT LAKE JUNALUSKA. Folkmoot USA, a two-week international folk festival hosted by Waynesville every summer has its closing grand finale in Stuart Auditorium. In 26 years, over 200 groups from more than 100 countries have performed in Haywood and nearby counties. (Courtesy of Folkmoot USA.)

Five

HAVING FUN AT LAKE JUNALUSKA

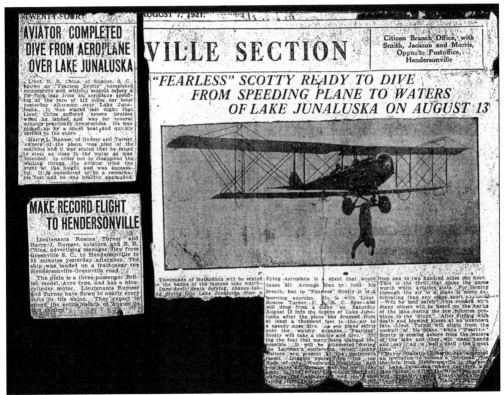

FEARLESS SCOTTY. In August 1921, the Layman's Conference witnessed a daredevil stunt when barnstorming B. R. "Fearless Scotty" China of Sumter, South Carolina, jumped into the lake from a speeding "aeroplane." The pilot misjudged the altitude and China let go at a higher level than usual. He was pulled from the lake badly bruised. Private camps, famous visitors, planned activities, and serendipitous events like the filming of a movie and airplane stunts have contributed to the Junaluska experience.

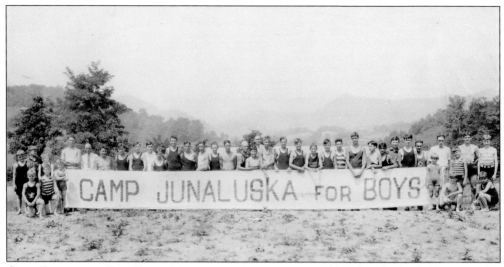

CAMP JUNALUSKA FOR BOYS. Numerous private camps utilized Junaluska facilities in the 1920s and 1930s. One of the most visible was the Junaluska Camp for Boys directed by Mason Crum, a summer resident for over 50 years. (Courtesy of Mason Crum papers, Duke University Archives.)

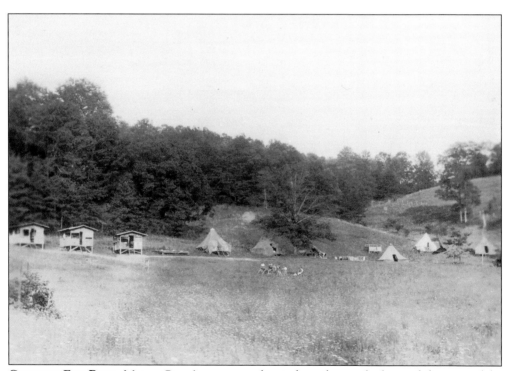

CAMPSITE FOR BOYS. Mason Crum's camp was located on the south shore of the upper lake between the narrows and Richland Creek. A professor of religion at Duke University, Crum employed university staff and students as directors and counselors. (Courtesy of Mason Crum papers, Duke University Archives.)

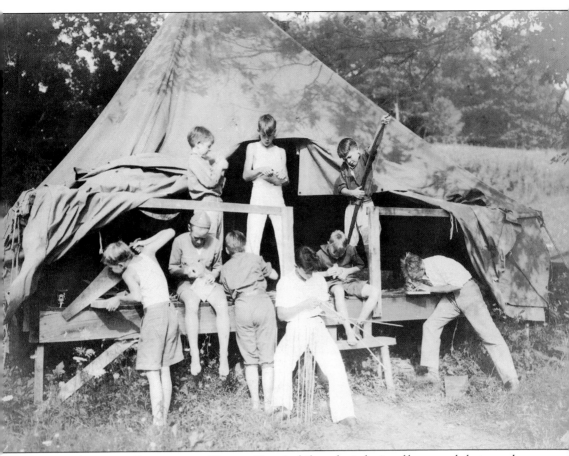

CAMPING ACTIVITIES ILLUSTRATED. Director Crum's philosophy is depicted by a posed photograph and caption reading, "The average boy delights in making things: a bow and arrow, a sun dial, a fireside motto, or what-not. He learns by doing. Character traits are learned by doing, by living the life; and the most effective teacher is a sympathetic friend and counselor." (Courtesy of Mason Crum papers, Duke University Archives.)

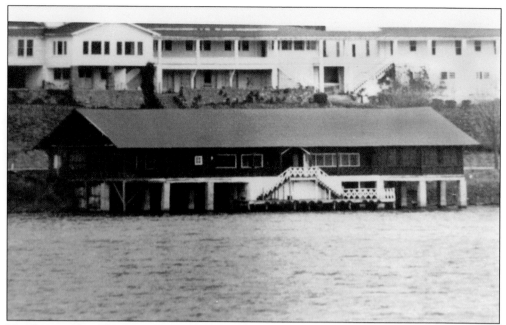

THE BOATHOUSE. The centrally located boathouse had rooms for instruction and Sunday school, a youth center for square dancing and to hang out, boats for rent, and a library and a tearoom for dining run by the Woman's Club.

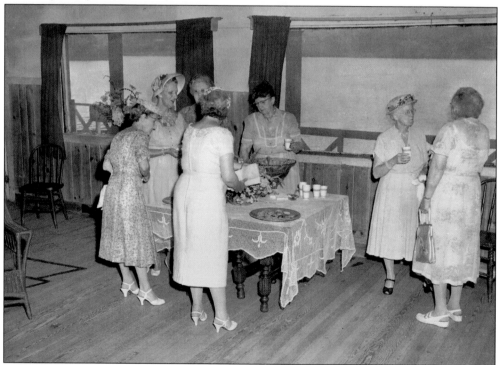

TEA IN THE BOATHOUSE. The Woman's Club, organized in 1917, sponsored vital social activities, maintained a library, tearoom, and a crafts program, as well as undertaking beautification projects. It played a major role in enhancing life during the summer season.

RUG HOOKING. The craft house had a full program of instruction including art, ceramics, and basket weaving. Here Mrs. L. E. Cogburn (seated) is instructing in rug hooking while Jane McDonald (left) and Mrs. Carl Mundy look on.

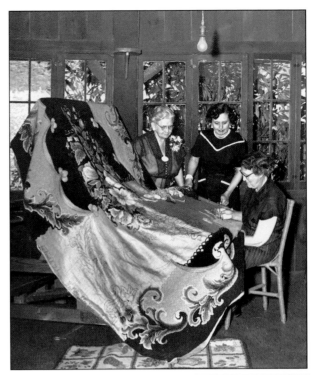

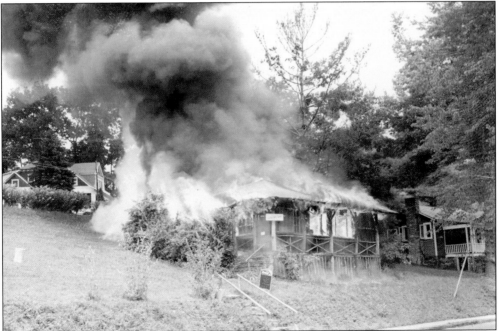

THE CRAFT HOUSE BURNS, 1958. The craft house of the Woman's Club, located between North Lakeshore and Chapel Drives, burned from an accidental kitchen fire in 1958. A larger, new craft facility named the Bransomb Arts and Crafts Building for Bishop John W. Branscomb was built near the Junaluska Apartments in 1960. Later it was relocated nearer the west gate and used for a variety of offices.

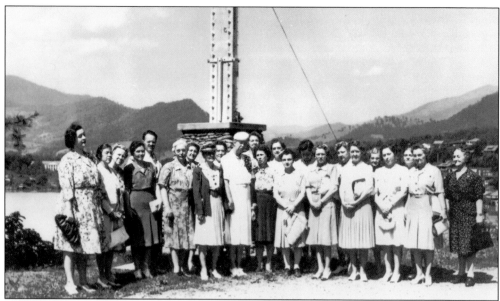

ELEANOR ROOSEVELT VISITS THE LAKE. Eleanor Roosevelt spent two days at Junaluska in July 1944, at a jurisdictional conference of the Woman's Society of Christian Service. She spoke to a full auditorium of 3,500 on issues facing a postwar world, including race relations. She had a full schedule, meeting with various groups from Haywood County as well. Roosevelt is tenth from the left. (Courtesy of Buddy Young.)

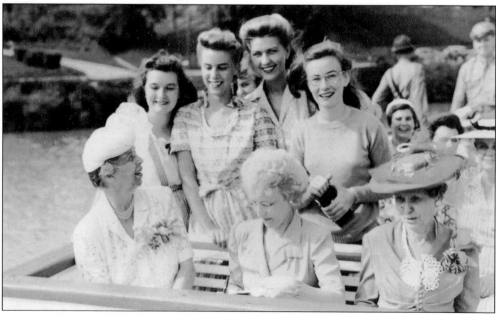

TERRACE WAITRESSES MEET ELEANOR ROOSEVELT. One day in July 1944, the cry, "Ride the Big Boat with Eleanor Roosevelt" rang out in the Terrace Hotel. The waitresses, resting between meals, rushed to meet the president's wife. Roosevelt (left) turns to speak to, from left to right, Peggy Herbert, Mary Crum, Kit Crum, and Skippy Herbert, who rushed out with her hair partially in curlers, not wanting to miss the occasion. The other women are unidentified. (Courtesy of Betty Chreitzburg Crenshaw.)

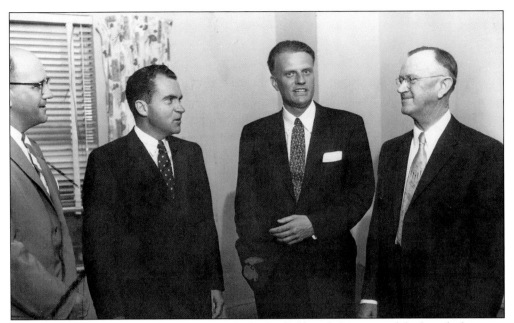

DISTINGUISHED VISITORS. Supt. James W. Fowler Jr. (left) and chairman of the board of trustees Edwin L. Jones (right) welcome Vice Pres. Richard M. Nixon and evangelist Billy Graham to the assembly in 1955. Graham, from nearby Black Mountain, preached at Junaluska for the first time in 1952 and at least six times altogether. (Courtesy of the *Mountaineer*.)

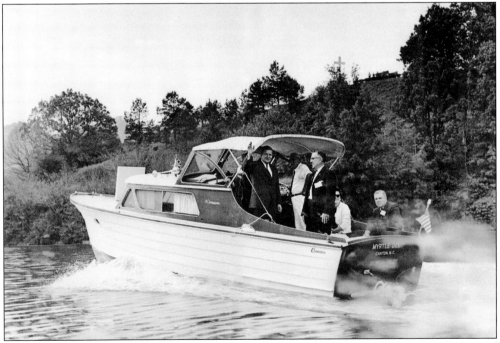

TERRY SANFORD. Terry Sanford (left), North Carolina governor, U.S. senator, president of Duke University, and a prominent Methodist layman, visited Junaluska frequently. While on a political visit leading a delegation from the state capital to western North Carolina in 1963, an executive from Champion Paper Company in Canton took him for a ride around the lake.

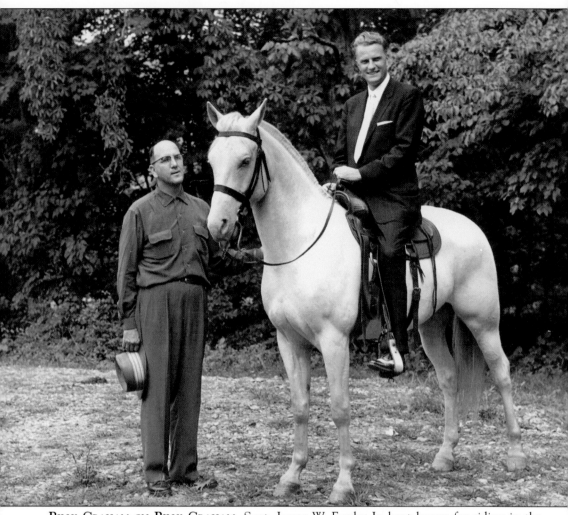

BILLY GRAHAM ON BILLY GRAHAM. Supt. James W. Fowler Jr. kept horses for riding in the off-season. He named one of his favorite mounts Billy Graham and could not resist introducing him to the real Billy Graham, who is seated atop his namesake. (Courtesy of Margaret Fowler McCleskey.)

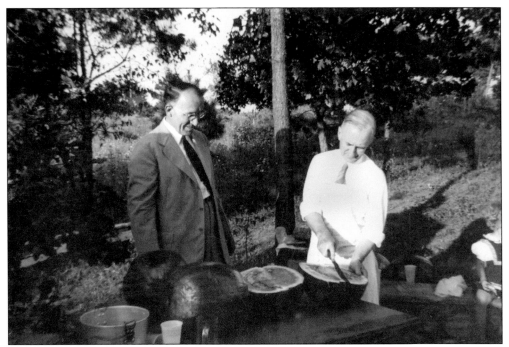

WATERMELON CUTTING. Outdoor cooking, making hand-churned ice cream, and watermelon cutting were favorite summer social events. Bishop Paul B. Kern (right) slices a watermelon for his neighbor, Benjamin H. Littleton. Judge Littleton, appointed to the Federal Court of Claims by Herbert Hoover, paid for the paving of the road by his house in 1948, which was given the name Littleton Road.

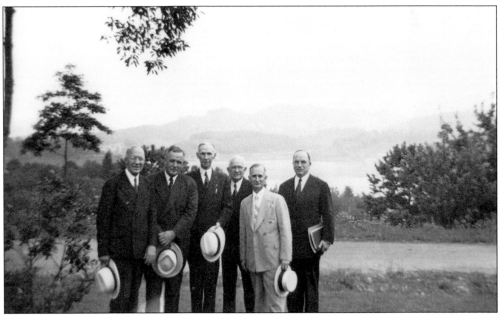

AFTER A PICNIC. Bishop Paul B. Kern, host (second from right), poses with his guests in front of his house in 1942. From left to right they are Bishops Arthur J. Moore, Hoyt M. Dobbs, Clare Purcell, W. W. Peele, and Bromley Oxnam.

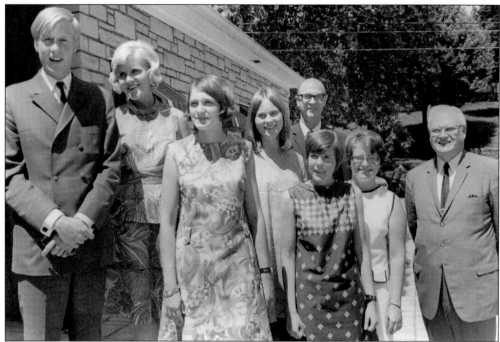

SCANDINAVIAN YOUTH VISIT. The Scandinavian Youth Caravan of 1968, hosted by Robert Stamey (in rear) and Bishop Earl G. Hunt (far right), visit the assembly. The Western North Carolina Conference and the Methodist Church in Scandinavia inaugurated an exchange program in 1955 in which teams visit each area every other year. Junaluska is always a stop for the international visitors. (Courtesy of the *Mountaineer*.)

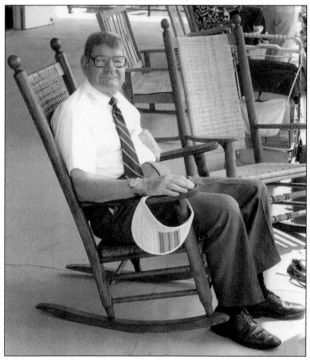

SAM McDONALD. Beloved longtime summer resident Sam McDonald could be found greeting people and rocking on the porch of the Harrell Center when not working in the Susan Todd Lounge. When he died, a half-dozen rockers were placed on the porch in his memory. (Courtesy of the *Mountaineer*.)

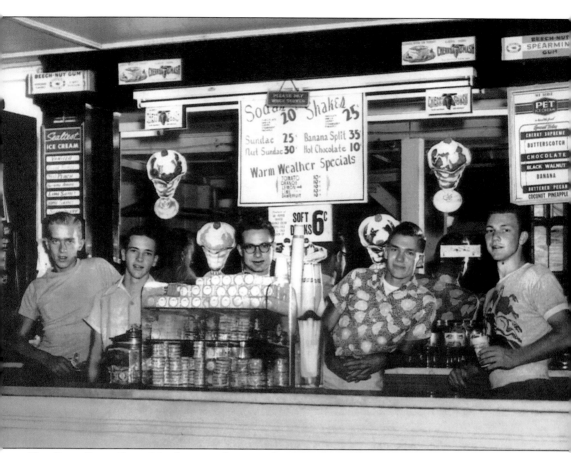

THE SODA SHOP. One of the favorite places on the grounds was the soda shop, which appealed to all ages. It was open until 11:00 p.m. but the jukebox on the screen porch overlooking the lake had to be turned off in the evening until the program in the auditorium next door was finished. The soda jerks in 1951 are, from left to right, Madison "Major" Crum, Alvin Cobb, James Hart, Paul Hardin, and Joe Hart. (Courtesy of Paul Hardin.)

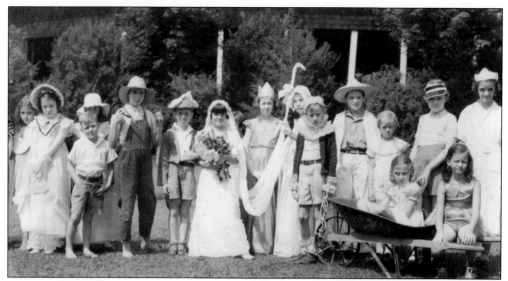

Storybook Characters. Little Bo Peep, Tom Sawyer, a queen and a court jester, a secretary, and a nurse are among the children in costume in this undated photograph outside Stuart Auditorium. Perhaps they were on their way, dressed as their favorite character, to the popular story hour in Stuart Auditorium conducted by John R. Pepper, denominational Sunday school leader and head of the board of trustees.

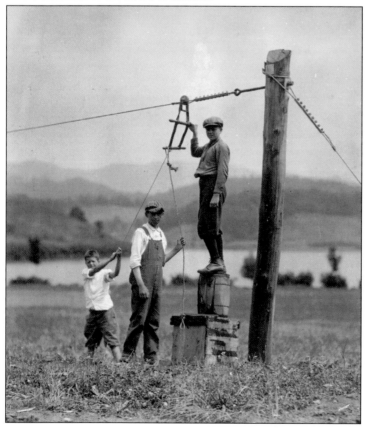

The Favorite Ride. This precursor to the modern zip line was the most popular source of enjoyment in the original playground in the 1920s. However, nervous adults did not replace it after the base of a support post rotted away over one winter.

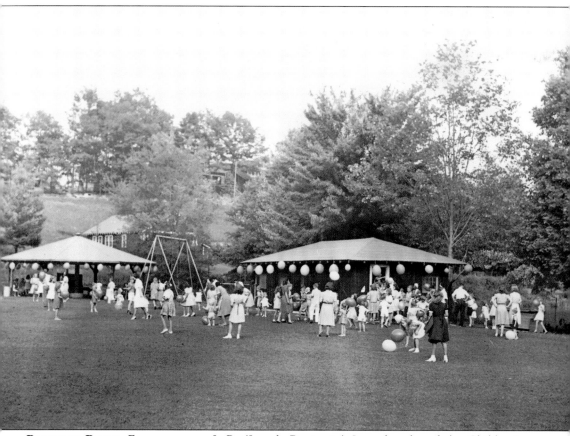

BIRTHDAY PARTY. Every summer, J. B. (Joseph Benjamin) Ivey, founder of the Children's Playground, staged a birthday party for the children at the lake complete with balloons, ice cream, entertainment, and even presents for everyone. Ivey opened a retail store in Charlotte, North Carolina, in 1900, which grew into the J. B. Ivey and Company department store chain in the Carolinas and Florida. Son of a Methodist minister and a staunch churchman, he had curtains lowered in the windows of his stores on Sunday so as not to advertise on the Lord's day.

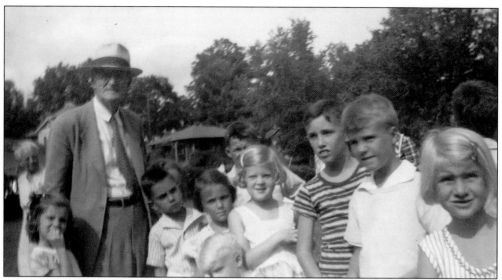

J. B. Ivey, c. 1946. J. B. Ivey, who built a home on North Lakeshore Drive in 1918, was a major presence at Junaluska for decades. Children usually followed wherever he went. Ivey is shown here with the following children, from left to right, from Littleton Road: unidentified, Ivey, Billy King, Libba Herbert, Peggy McLarty, unidentified, Frank Jordan, and Janet Jordan. Bobby Dick Jordan is partially visible in the front. (Courtesy of Frank Jordan.)

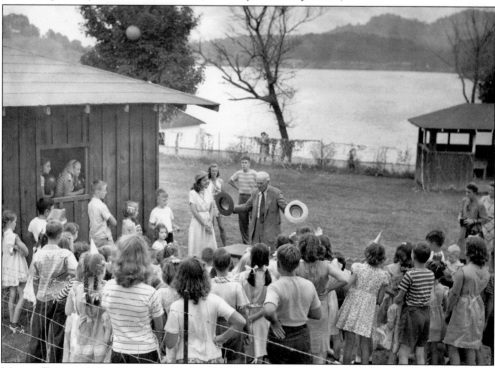

Magic Tricks. J. B. Ivey always enthralled a crowd with magic tricks. He also delighted in growing dahlias and gladiolas on the corner lot of Littleton Road and North Lakeshore Drive near his home. His flower garden provided arrangements for Stuart Auditorium and pleasure for anyone who picked up free flowers he set out in cans every morning.

FISHING. Sam Williams shows off a big catch from the lake in 1959. Fish and birds were plentiful for years, but when the removal of silt and draining the lake for repairs on the dam became a necessity, large catches were fewer. Documented water pollution in the late 1940s turned much needed attention to upstream conditions surrounding Richland Creek, the main tributary for the lake.

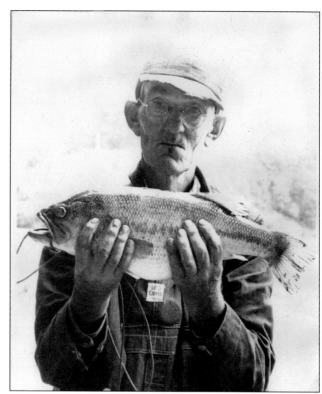

KISSMISKOLCZ. *The Swan*, a 1956 MGM motion picture starring Grace Kelly and Alec Guinness was filmed at the nearby Biltmore Estate. The Junaluska train station was used for the scene where the visiting prince arrives to meet the royal family in this romantic comedy set in Europe. (Courtesy of Donald H. Mosley.)

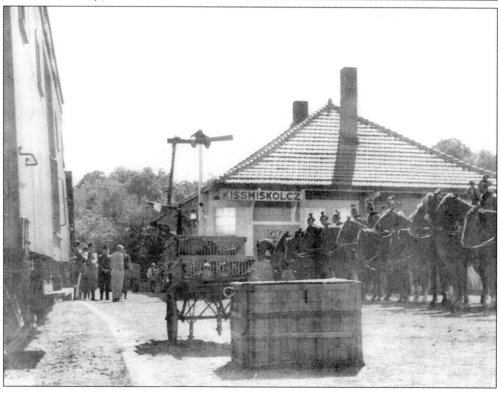

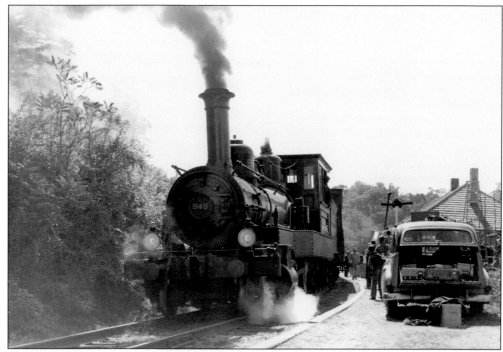

MAKING A MOVIE. Seeking authenticity, the motion picture set of *The Swan* included an 1888 Baltimore and Ohio locomotive towed from Maryland to North Carolina for the scene filmed at Junaluska.

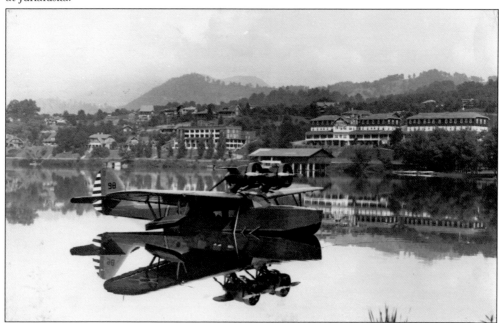

A MODERN AIRPLANE. The J. A. Baylor family from Wytheville, Virginia, built one of the original houses at the lake, and J. A. Baylor designed Lambuth Inn. His son, Joe Baylor, a pilot in the U.S. Army Aviation Corps, created much excitement when he dropped in for a visit with his parents in 1931.

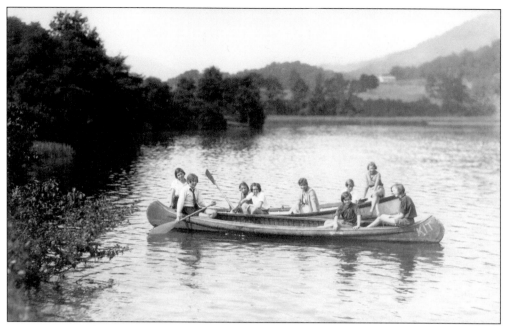

BOATING. Friends meet around a canoe named for one of Mason Crum's daughters. Boating styles changed over the years, with the Sunfish sailboat and the paddleboat becoming popular. Speedboat races were held in the 1950s but were later banned in favor of a quieter sanctuary. (Courtesy of Mason Crum papers, Duke University Archives.)

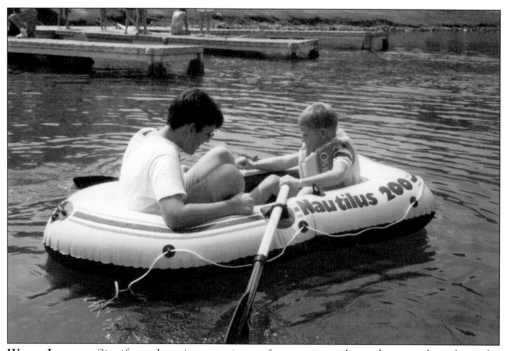

WATER LESSONS. Significant learning experiences for young people on the water have been the first dive off the high diving board and learning to maneuver a boat. Matt McCleskey (left) gives Burns Aldridge his first rowing lesson. (Courtesy of Margaret Fowler McCleskey.)

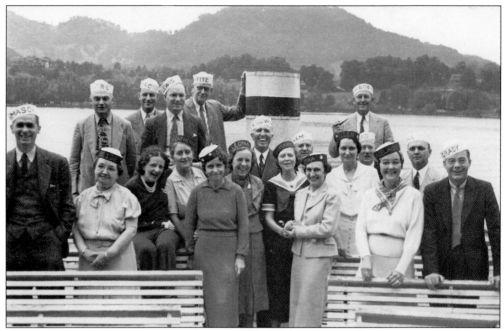

CHAPLAIN'S PARTY, 1938. Adm. William N. Thomas (center, in front of the fake smokestack) hosts a party on the second deck of *Cherokee I*. Thomas, a homeowner and dean of the chapel, was an authentic admiral as chief of navy chaplains. (Courtesy of Mason Crum papers, Duke University Archives.)

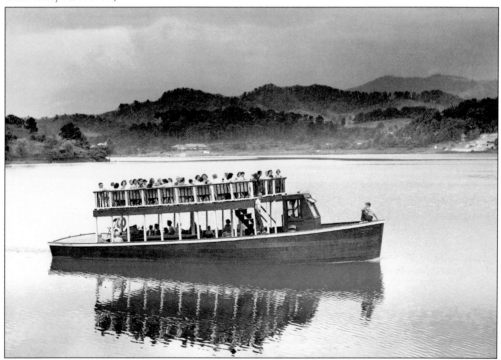

CHEROKEE II. *Cherokee I*, the Big Boat, plied the waters doing yeoman work for 37 years. Its successor, *Cherokee II*, was the tour boat from 1951 to 1967.

CHEROKEE III. *Cherokee III*, a strange-looking vessel, served from 1967 to 1997. Most everyone preferred the scenery from the second deck, which often gave *Cherokee III* a list unless the riders were properly distributed.

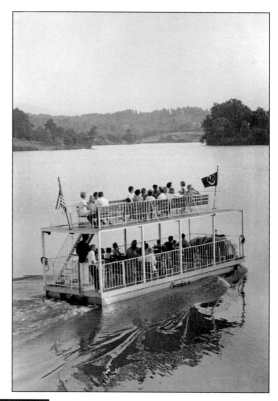

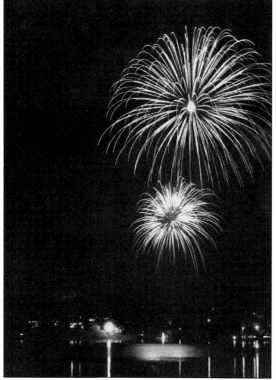

JULY 4TH. In the early days, July 4th was celebrated with a covered dish picnic on the grounds and a speaker in Stuart Auditorium, but it has acquired an increasingly full agenda through the years. The fireworks display, the largest in Haywood County, draws thousands of spectators, who fill the road around the lake. (Courtesy of the *Mountaineer.*)

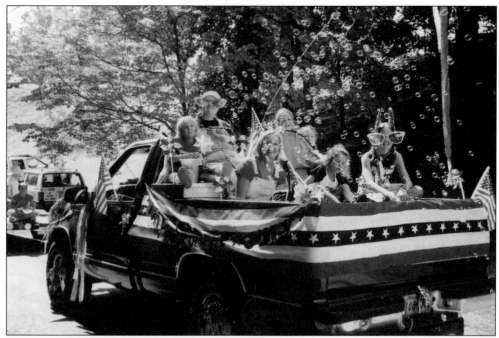

A Unique Parade. In the late 1950s, boat and swim races gave way to a parade to celebrate the 4th of July. Friends, family, and staff participate in a unique parade that anyone can join. Family reunions make the holiday one of the busiest times of the year. Here young members of the Herbert family join the fun. (Courtesy of J. Hughes Roberts Jr.)

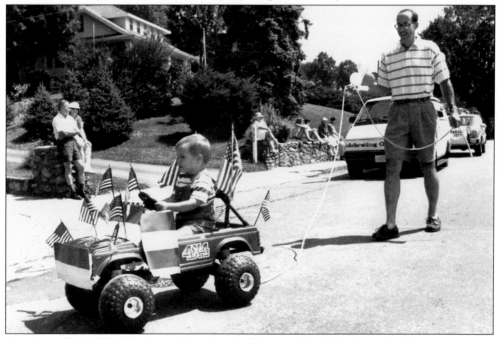

All Ages. Daniel G. Martin, minister in the Western North Carolina Conference, attempts to keep his two-year-old son, Parker, under control during a 4th of July parade. (Courtesy of the *Mountaineer*.)

Six

RECREATION AND YOUTH ACTIVITIES

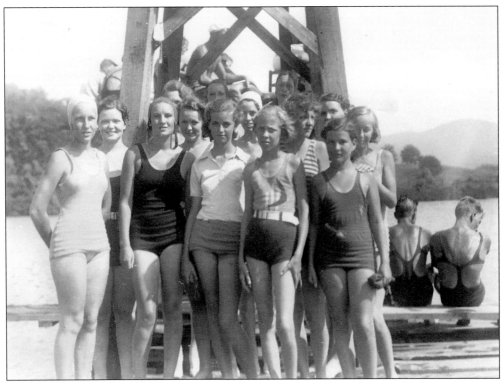

CAMPS HAD THEIR OWN PIERS. Recreational activities were varied but usually centered on the lake. Swimming occurred at several places in the lake as some private camps had their own piers and water activities. Some 6–10 private camps operated on and around the grounds before the Depression, World War II, and a polio epidemic made them unprofitable. However, the need for updated and new facilities was ever present. After World War II, an increase in family camping created the need for another type of campground. (Courtesy of Mason Crum papers, Duke University Archives.)

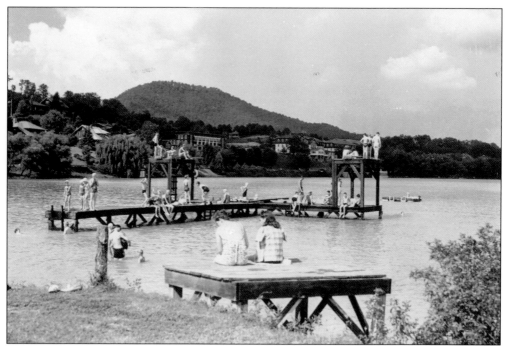

SWIMMING IN THE LAKE. A permanent rock bathhouse was constructed in 1946 to upgrade swimming facilities. A polio epidemic restricted activity and reduced the number of young people at the lake for a few years in the late 1940s. Health inspectors closed the lake to swimming for sanitary reasons in 1953.

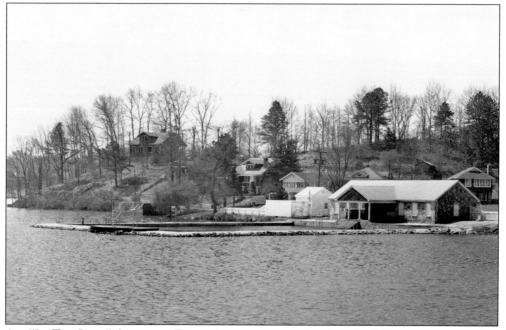

AN "IN THE LAKE" SWIMMING POOL. A swimming pool within the lake was constructed in 1954 to deal with continuing health concerns. Swimming on Sunday afternoon was permitted in 1963. A new bathhouse and swimming pool replaced the original ones in 1995.

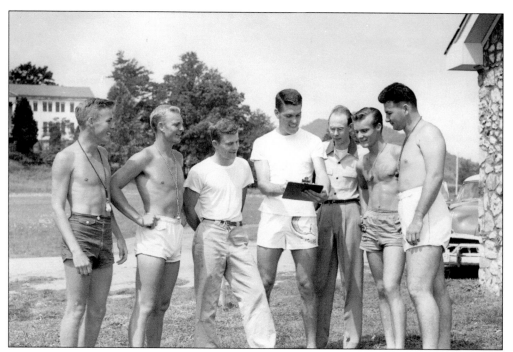

A Comprehensive Recreation Program. Richard J. "Dick" Crowder, a divinity school student at Duke University, was employed as director of recreation from 1950 to 1952. Shown here is the staff for 1951. From left to right are Tom Stockton, Joe Jack Wells, Bill Royster, Crowder, Dwight Pyatt, Dave Herbert, and J. D. "Tank" Lawrence. Pyatt was director of religious education, and the others had responsibilities as lifeguards and in recreation. (Courtesy of Richard J. Crowder.)

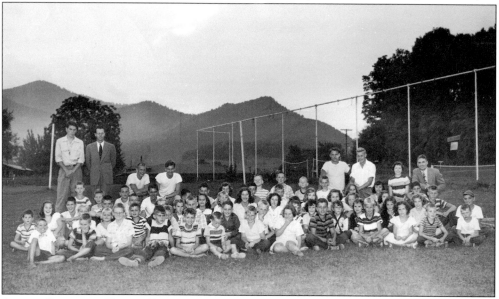

Active Clubs for Youth. Recognizing a need for organized activities, Dick Crowder created boys and girls clubs for resident and local area youth. Pictured here in 1952 are 60 youth who participated in a variety of sports, camping, and religious activities. They tried to have one overnight camping experience a week. (Courtesy of Richard J. Crowder.)

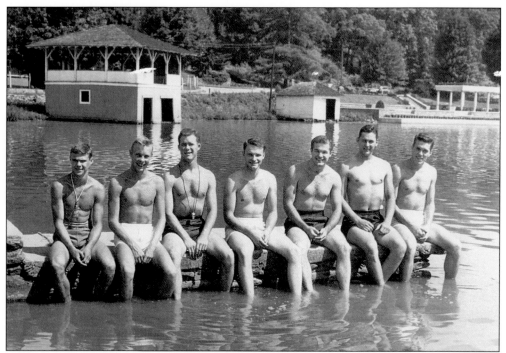

LIFEGUARDS IN 1952. Lifeguards in 1952 were, from left to right, Morton Carl, Tom Stockton, Art O'Neil, Bill Lewis, John Carey, Tom Wood, and Richard Crowder. Note the type of private boathouses that dotted the lake along North Lakeshore Drive. (Courtesy of Richard J. Crowder.)

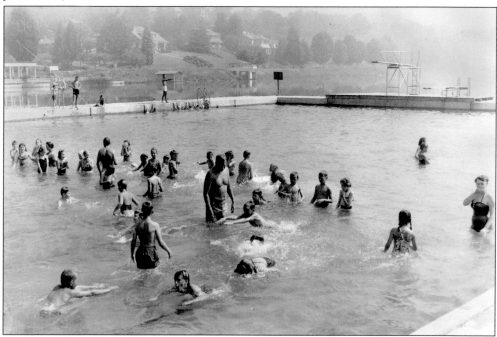

WATER SAFETY. Hundreds of resident and area youth learned how to swim and water safety in addition to earning lifesaving certification as part of youth activities through the years.

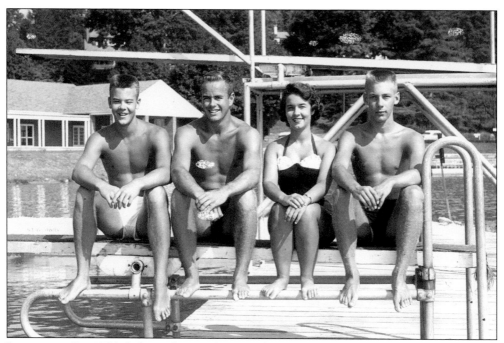

Lifeguards In 1956. Lifeguards in 1956 were, from left to right, Richard Beauchamp, Carl Mundy, Carol Thornton, and Melford Wilson Jr. (Courtesy of Melford A. Wilson Jr.)

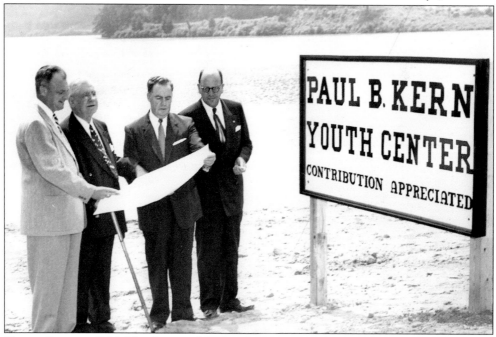

Youth Center, 1956. The demise of the boathouse created the need for a youth center. Here are, from left to right, Sam Banks, chair of the youth activities committee board of trustees; Bishop Charles Selecman, friend and colleague of Kern; Lee F. Tuttle, fund campaign director; and James W. Fowler Jr., superintendent, launching the financial campaign to raise money for the new building, which was named after the late Paul B. Kern.

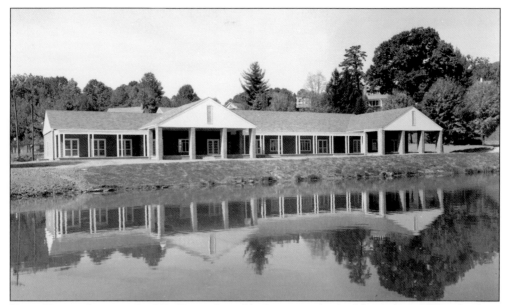

KERN YOUTH CENTER. Paul B. Kern, elected bishop in 1930, had been dean of the theology department at Southern Methodist University and minister to churches in Tennessee and Texas. Recognizing Kern, who believed nurturing youth built the church of the future and that the Junaluska experience was a prime example of that nurture, was appropriate. His Episcopal assignments were to East Asia (China, Korea, Japan), four conferences in the Carolinas, and the Tennessee area, which included Florida and Cuba. He built a home at Junaluska in 1940.

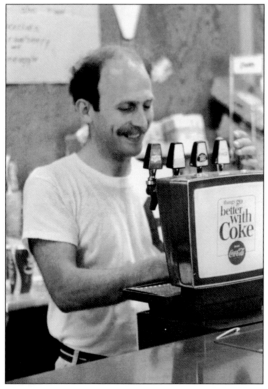

A NEW SODA SHOP. The Kern Youth Center continued the tradition of a soda shop, now called the Kern Kafe. Here Frank Buckner, grandson of Bishop Kern, dispenses a drink in 1980. The building was in a recreation complex that contained tennis and shuffleboard courts, a multipurpose ball field, a swimming pool, and an area for small boat rental.

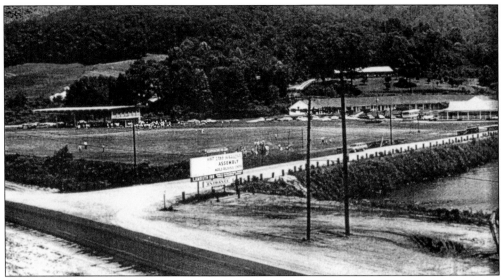

A GYMNASIUM. The enhanced recreational facilities lacked a basketball court. When Nanci Weldon, summer resident, former queen of Junaluska, and recent graduate of Duke University, died at an early age of cancer in 1965, a memorial fund was established in her honor. The fund was used to construct a gymnasium, open on three sides, near the west gate, viewed here on the left.

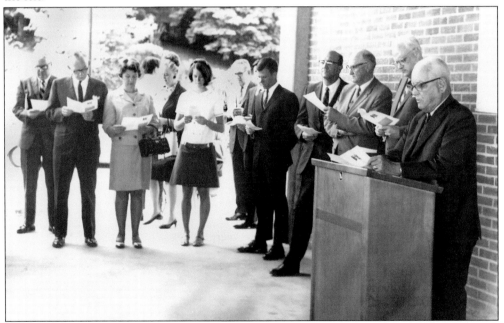

NANCI WELDON GYM. Participants at the June 1969 dedication of the Nanci Weldon Memorial Gymnasium are Nanci's parents, Wilson and Margaret Weldon (first row, left); siblings Alice and Bill Weldon (third and fourth from left in first row); Jim Fowler, Hugh Massey, Bishop Hunt, and Frank Smathers. The dedication program reprinted remarks Nanci Weldon had made when she was crowned queen, noting, "I just hope [Junaluska] will continue to grow to become a place where the social classes and castes of the old South are forgotten but where the Southern charm, friendliness, and hospitality are preserved."

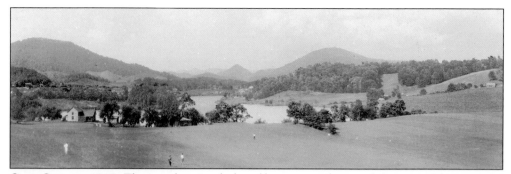

GOLF COURSE, 1919. The popular nine-hole golf course southwest of the upper lake occupied attractive acreage. Trustees considered selling the land when assembly debt rose in the 1920s, and Haywood County had to be persuaded to look elsewhere when it selected the site for a new consolidated high school in 1963. The course was expanded to 18 holes in the mid-1990s.

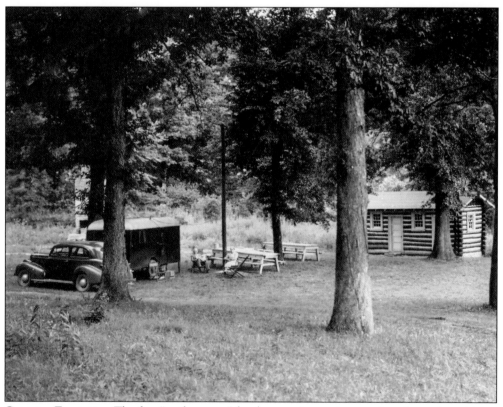

CAMPING FACILITIES. The first "trailer camp" for the ever-increasing number of travelers visiting by automobile opened in 1939. Located on the east side of the golf course, it boasted electricity to attract campers.

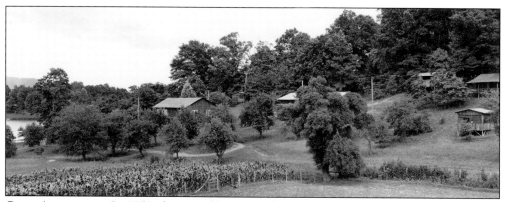

CAMP ADVENTURE. In 1950, the assembly acquired Camp Adventure, a private coeducational camp that had used Junaluska facilities since 1941. The assembly moved its tent and trailer camp to this expanded location.

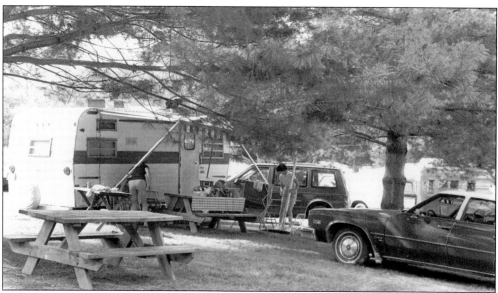

AUTOMOTIVE CAMPING. The postwar car culture and consequent increase in family camping made tent and trailer camping a popular alternative for assembly guests, as well as for the traveling public. Here Roland and Emilie Barnhardt set up for an extended stay at Lake Junaluska. (Courtesy of the *Mountaineer*.)

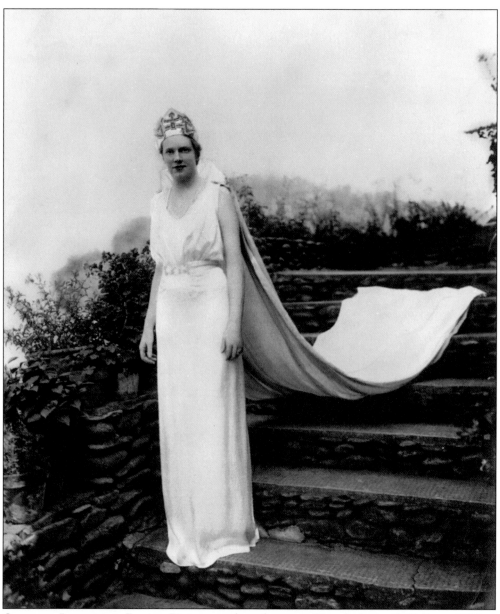

QUEEN OF JUNALUSKA. Frances Bivins was elected queen of Junaluska in 1935. From 1922 to 1977, the focus of end-of-the-summer youth activities was the election of a queen. The queen was chosen from current staff members or residents, and the criteria for the nomination were character, participation in activities, and beauty.

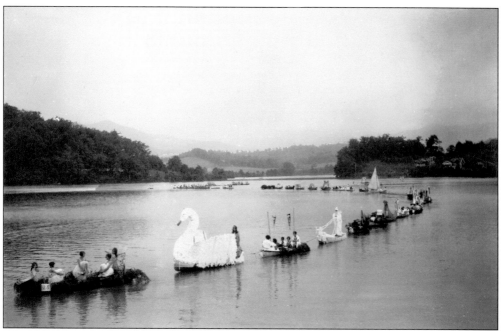

THE BOAT PAGEANT. In the 1920s, the Junaluska queen was initially called the "Queen of the Boat Pageant." A long line of tableaus mounted on boats, pulled by *Cherokee I*, formed the pageant.

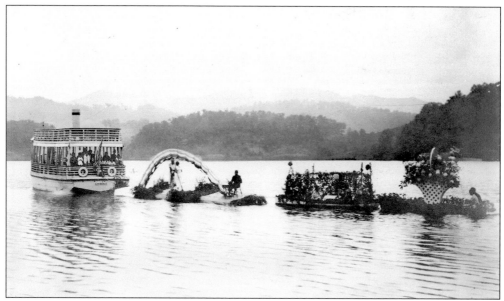

A THEMED BOAT PARADE. The line of decorated boats usually followed a theme, such as illustrating nursery rhymes. Silver cups were awarded for the best idea and the most attractive displays. The coronation in Stuart Auditorium was the final event of several days of special activity.

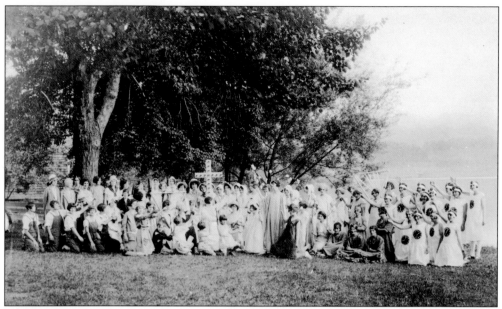

THE CORONATION CEREMONY. Pageant participants from the 1926 coronation ceremony pose outside Stuart Auditorium. Coronation pageants involved all ages and followed a carefully planned script for a full evening of entertainment.

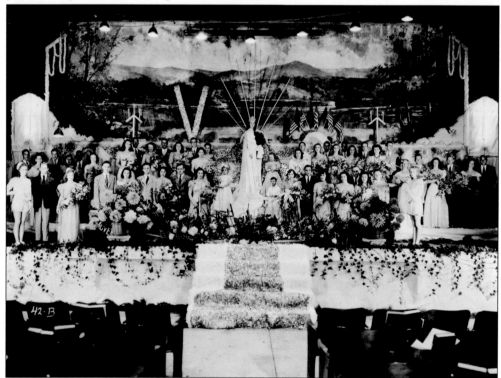

A WARTIME THEME. The wartime coronation of Louise Holcomb in 1942 had a patriotic theme. Themes varied from musical reviews of the day to historical subjects to commemorating appropriate events of a particular year.

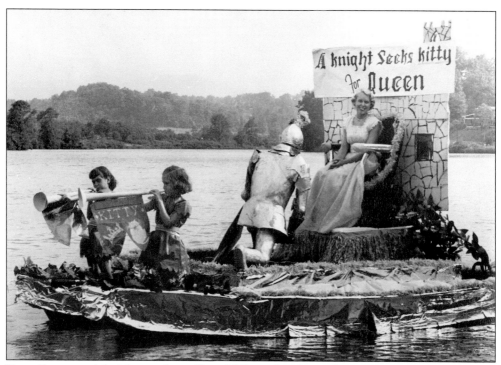

BOAT PARADES. A knight proclaims Kitty Miller as his choice for queen in 1951. Towed boats were used as platforms for scenes in campaigns for queen. Each candidate had a campaign manager who orchestrated her campaign. (Courtesy of Kitty Miller Coble.)

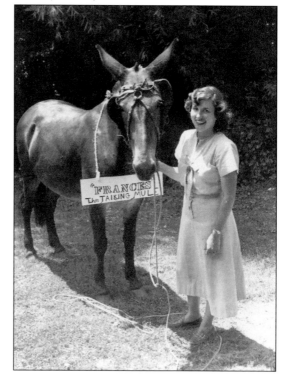

LANDLUBBERS CREATIVITY. One of the more ingenious campaign displays occurred in 1950 when James Hart tied a "talking mule" by Lakeshore Drive. He rigged a speaker to repeat, "Vote for Frances Cobb" when activated in the soda shop. Reticent bishop Costen J. Harrell was not amused when "Frances the Talking Mule" asked for his vote. Frances Cobb is pictured here with the mule. (Courtesy of James Hart.)

113

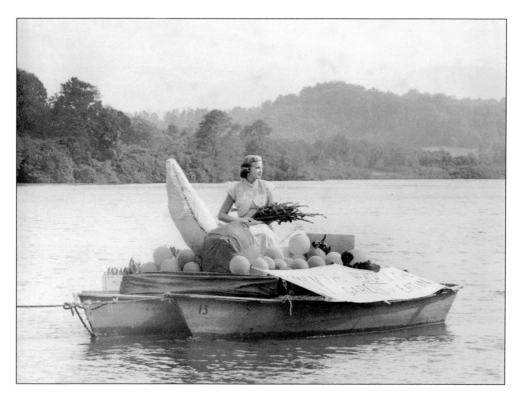

INDIVIDUAL FLOATS. Nancy Hobbs' float (above) in 1951 identified her as "The Peach in the Garden of Eatin'." Lucy Neeley used the popular television show *I Love Lucy* as her boat theme in 1953. (Above, courtesy of Nancy Hobbs Banks; below, courtesy of Lucy Neeley Adams.)

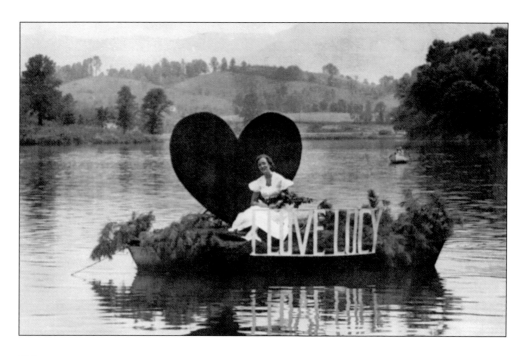

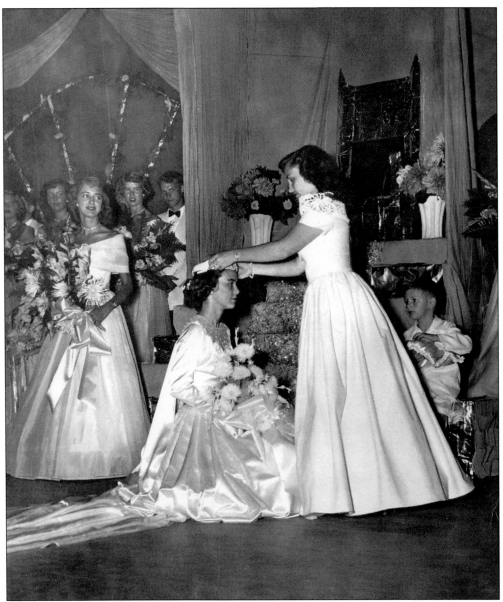

PASSING THE CROWN. Frances Cobb (right) crowns Barbara Russell queen in 1951. Each of these queens was from a longtime resident family committed to the ideals and purpose of the assembly. Each in turn married members of likewise committed families; Frances married James Hart and Barbara married Paul Hardin.

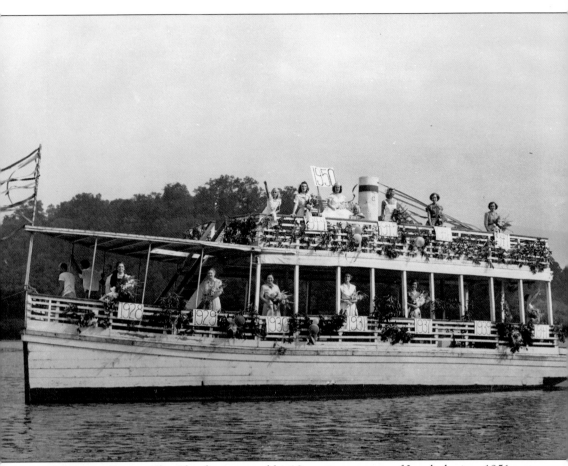

A Unique Cargo. The *Cherokee* is graced by 10 previous queens of Junaluska in a 1951 water pageant. The array of queens added interest to the boat, clearly showing its age. (Courtesy of James Hart.)

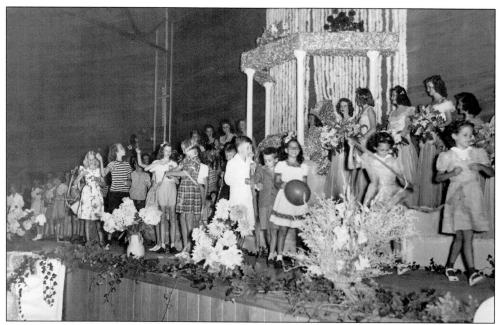

CHILDREN ENTERTAIN THE QUEEN. Children solicited from activities at the Ivey Playground always had a part in the coronation ceremony. Here they provide entertainment for queen Kit Crum in 1945. (Courtesy of Beaman Griffin.)

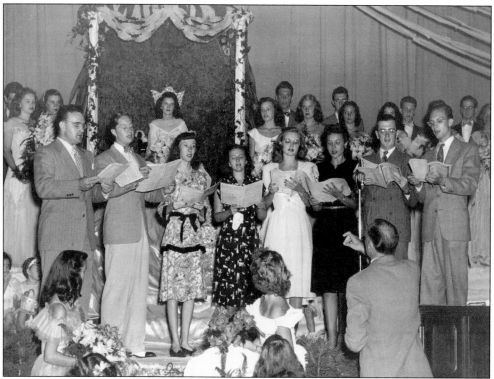

SINGERS ENTERTAIN. Queen Polly Dyer is serenaded by eight singers directed by Alec Siwson in 1947.

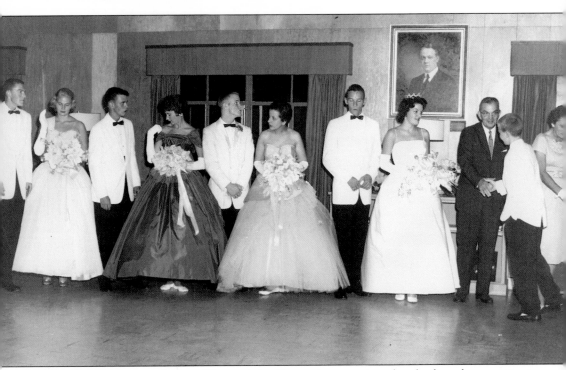

THE RECEIVING LINE BEGINS. The receiving line at the reception after the formal coronation in 1959 included, from left to right, Lem Wiggins; Margaret Brugger; Steve Beauchamp; Gretchen Bartlet; Clyde Chase; Eleanor Barksdale; Brother Carter; the queen, Mary Harriet Wiggins; and her parents, Lemuel Wiggins II and Alice Holler Wiggins. The young boy is unidentified. (Courtesy of Mary Harriet Wiggins Carter.)

A Special Guest, 1962. The 1961 outgoing queen Nanci Weldon (left) crowns Martha Russell queen in 1962, with Maria Beale Fletcher looking on. Fletcher, the reigning Miss America, was from nearby Asheville, North Carolina.

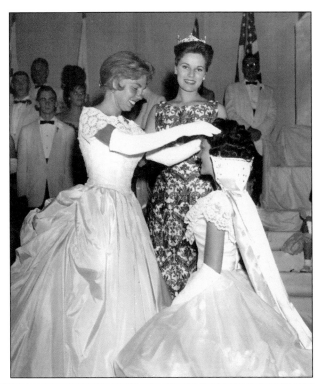

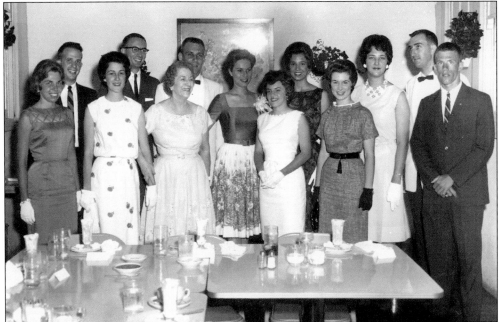

A Formal. Proper Southern ladies host a dinner for Miss America, Maria Beale Fletcher. Attending, from left to right, were Nanci Weldon, unidentified, Martha Russell, Wannamaker Hardin, an unidentified woman who is possibly Maria Beale Fletcher's mother, Melford Wilson, Maria Beale Fletcher, two unidentified women, Sara Evans, Margaret Fowler, Lawrence McCleskey, and Bill Weldon.

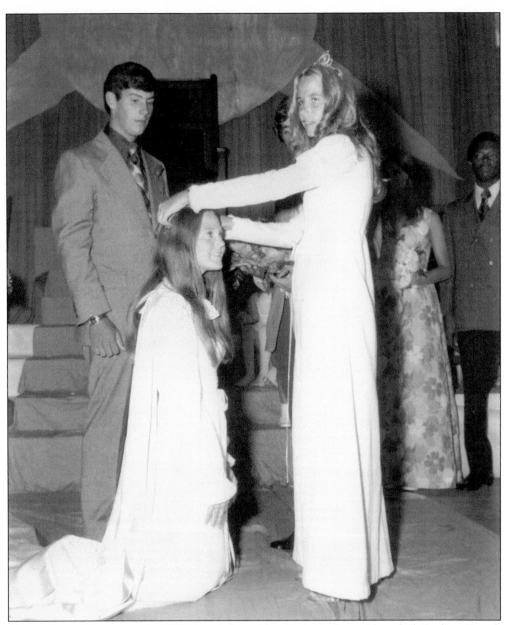

QUEEN SUSAN ANDERSON. In 1972, from left to right, Andy Banks, unidentified, Carlene Kessel, and Sammy Jackson witness Elodie Hale crown Susan Anderson queen. Across the country, institutions of all kinds were questioned in the 1970s, and the election of a queen at Junaluska did not escape scrutiny. Coronations became simpler affairs. In 1973, the only African American queen, Sylvia Ann Harkness, and the only king, Fred McWhorter, were crowned. Apparently no official photographer recorded the coronation in 1973. The last queen was Ross Ann Haire in 1977. (Courtesy of Susan Anderson Wiggins.)

Seven

HOMES WITH A STORY

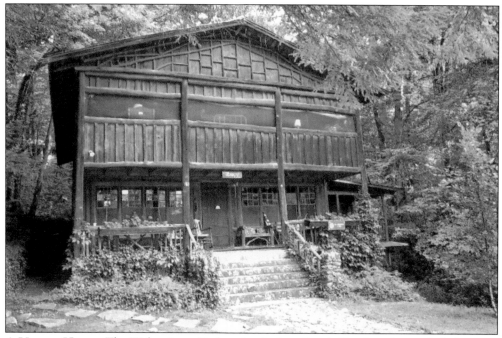

A Unique House. The Walter Isaac Herbert family from South Carolina dreamed of a house at Junaluska but could only afford a lot, hoping to build in the future. Excited to be at Junaluska, the family was camping in a tent on their lot when George R. Stuart noted their plight one rainy summer and offered them the use of a nearby house he was building. They bought the house in 1919 and the Adirondack-style house at 767 County Road has been kept in its original state. (Photograph by Marie Metcalf.)

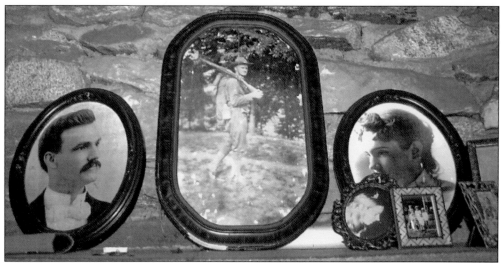

THOMAS CARLISLE HERBERT. The means for Walter Isaac (left) and Constance Furman Herbert to own a house sadly developed when their son, Thomas Carlisle Herbert, died of influenza in France while serving in World War I. He left a modest inheritance through an insurance policy, which was used for the purchase. Pictures on the mantel depict Thomas Carlisle Herbert (center), and his parents. (Photograph by Marie Metcalf.)

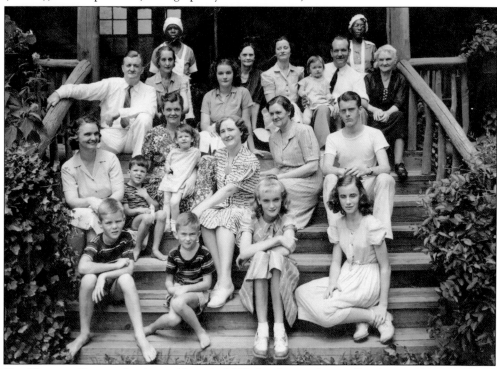

THE HERBERT FAMILY. As pictured here in 1940, family members still gather on the steps for an annual photograph. Succeeding generations of the Herbert family have continued to keep the house by a unique arrangement. It is owned by six family units who share expenses and pay a daily stipend for maintenance when using it. One member is the designated gatekeeper to keep everything in order. (Courtesy of J. Hughes Roberts Jr.)

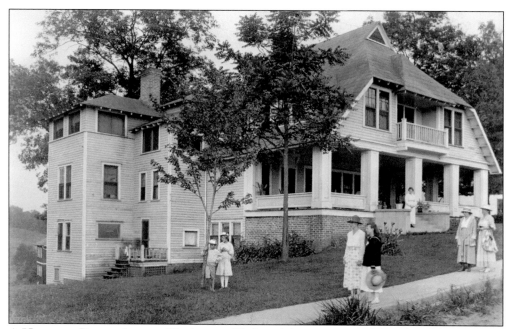

A Home for Bishop Atkins. The home of Bishop Atkins, a principal founder of the Southern Assembly, is located at 979 North Lakeshore Drive. There is some question as to how much he actually lived in this summerhouse because of the illness and death of his wife, Ella Branner Atkins. It was leased in 1914 for use as a boardinghouse. Atkins already had a house nearby in his hometown of Waynesville. Known today as Sunset Inn, its ambiance remains true to its original state.

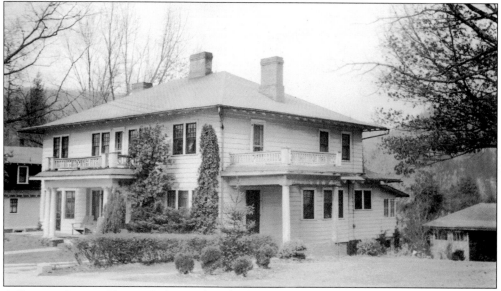

A Second Atkins House. Bishop Atkins built a home for his second wife, Eva Rose Atkins, next door to his first home at 959 North Lakeshore Drive. Mrs. Atkins donated the house to the assembly for a residence for the superintendent in 1944. When a modern home was built in 1965 for the superintendent on Cokesbury Circle, Mrs. Odille Ousley purchased the house and gave it to the assembly. Today it serves as the Intentional Growth Center.

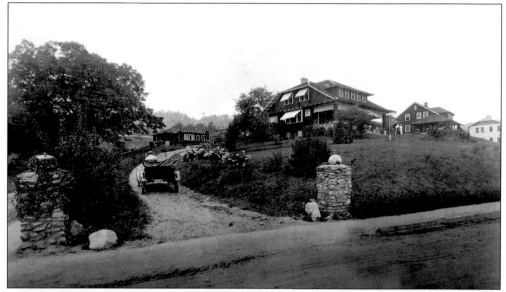

WINONA. George R. Stuart first envisioned a Methodist assembly in the South while visiting the religious assembly at Winona Lake in northeastern Indiana in the 1890s. He named his 489 North Lakeshore Drive home Winona.

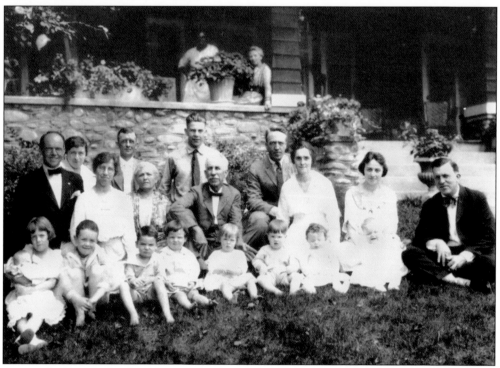

GEORGE R. STUART. Pictured here with his family, George R. Stuart (center) was a Presbyterian before becoming a Methodist as a young man. He had successful pastorates in Tennessee and Alabama but enjoyed evangelistic work most. The evangelist Sam Jones invited Stuart to join him, launching Stuart's own career as a revivalist and Chautauqua speaker. He was also an effective speaker in the temperance movement.

THE HOLLER'S RAINBOW COTTAGE. There are three Sears Roebuck and Company mail order houses on the grounds, one of which was built by Adlai Elwood Holler of Clio, South Carolina, in 1913. The house kits were ordered out of a catalogue, shipped by railroad, and hauled on site by wagon to be assembled. Four children pitched in to help assemble the house at 846 County Road. (Courtesy of Marian Rice Sigman.)

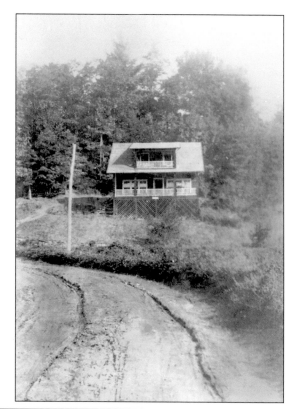

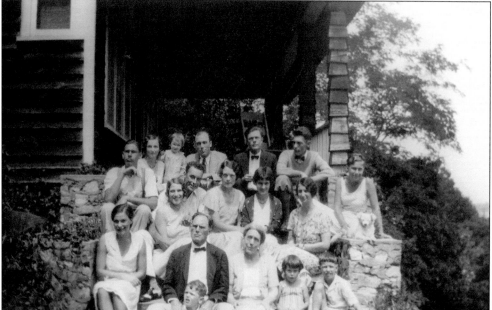

THE HOLLER FAMILY. Adlai E. and Mary "May" C. Holler (first row, center) pose with their eight children and grandchildren on the steps of their cottage in the early 1930s. A family member estimates extended family members through several generations have had 21 houses at Junaluska. They have been holding reunions at Junaluska since 1939. (Courtesy of Melford A. Wilson Jr.)

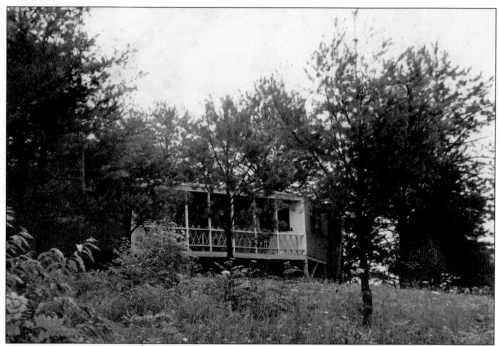

THE EMMETT K. MCLARTY FAMILY. After World War II, Emmett K. McLarty, a young minister in the Western North Carolina Conference, purchased two square surplus military housing units from Oak Ridge Tennessee, delivered on site for $75 each. He placed the units apart at an angle with a screen porch connecting them. The resulting three sections were named Mack Shack, Lean Back, and To-Bed-We-Go, according to their use. (Courtesy of Sallie Gordon McLarty.)

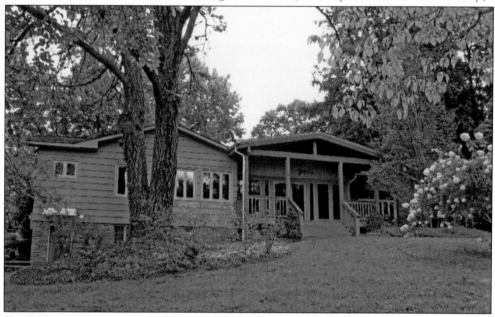

THE MCLARTY REPLACEMENT. Emmett McLarty learned stone masonry and built a permanent house on roughly the same floor plan. Today Boyd and Jean McLarty Holliday own the house at 29 Bomac Road. (Photograph by Marie Metcalf.)

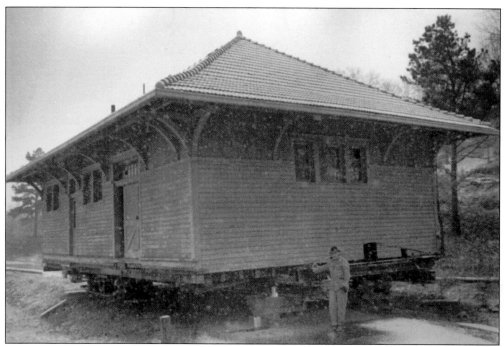

THE TRAIN STATION, 1969. Mr. and Mrs. Elmore Bailey of Ocala, Florida, bought the train station in 1969. The Baileys made plans to move it a quarter mile for a home by the lake. They discovered that the estimated 40-ton building weighed closer to 100 tons due to the tile roof when the moving truck broke down in the middle of the street. Snow and below zero temperature further complicated the move. After attractively fixing the station for personal living, the Baileys sold the house to Bishop Edward L. Tullis in 1976. (Courtesy of the *Mountaineer*.)

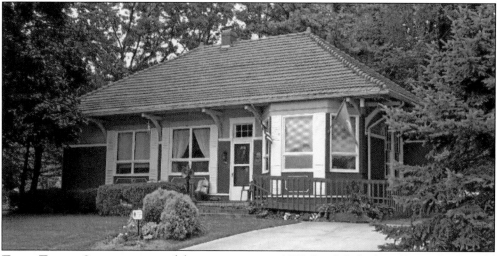

TRAIN THEME. Current owners of the train station at 1799 South Lakeshore Drive, Dr. Donald Mosley and his wife, Charlotte, of Louisville, Kentucky, live with the train motif daily. Their kitchen is the former ticket office, eating nook the telegraph station, living room the waiting room, and family room and two bedrooms the baggage room. The telegraph key sits on the kitchen counter and the ticket window serves as a pass-through. The orange tile roof is still original. (Photograph by Marie Metcalf.)

DISCOVER THOUSANDS OF LOCAL HISTORY BOOKS FEATURING MILLIONS OF VINTAGE IMAGES

Arcadia Publishing, the leading local history publisher in the United States, is committed to making history accessible and meaningful through publishing books that celebrate and preserve the heritage of America's people and places.

Find more books like this at
www.arcadiapublishing.com

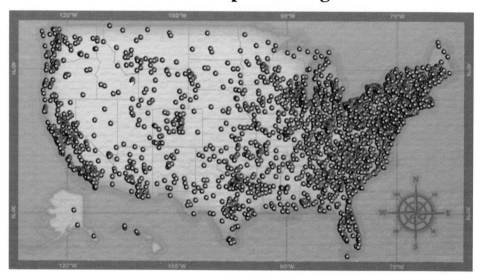

Search for your hometown history, your old stomping grounds, and even your favorite sports team.

 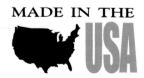